THE CREATIVE GUIDE TO

FABRIC
SCREEN PRINTING

THE CREATIVE GUIDE TO

FABRIC
SCREEN PRINTING

Pam Stallebrass

NH
NEW
HOLLAND

First published in the UK in 1990 by New Holland (Publishers) Ltd
37 Connaught Street, London W2 2AZ

Reprinted in 1992

ISBN 1 85368 126 1 (hardback)
ISBN 1 85368 217 9 (paperback)

Editor: Valerie Fourie
Designer: Jenny Camons
Cover Designer: Jenny Camons
Photographers: Pam Stallebrass,
Alain Proust and Herschel Mair
Illustrator: Pam Stallebras

Phototypeset by Studiographix CC
Reproduction by Unifoto (Pty) Ltd
Printed and bound in Hong Kong by Leefung-Asco Printers Ltd

All the projects featured in this book were designed and printed using metric measurements.
If, however, you prefer to follow the imperial measurements which appear in square brackets,
please remember that most conversions have been rounded off to the nearest $\frac{1}{8}$ inch
- sometimes up and sometimes down, depending on which is more appropriate.
Where a more accurate conversion is important, it has been given. (For example,
a 2 mm overlap is converted to $\frac{1}{12}$ in.)

*(Previous spread, left) Alive with colour and distinctly individual, the author's holiday cottage
illustrates the effective application of home-printed fabrics. (Right) A medley of Ndebele designs.*

CONTENTS

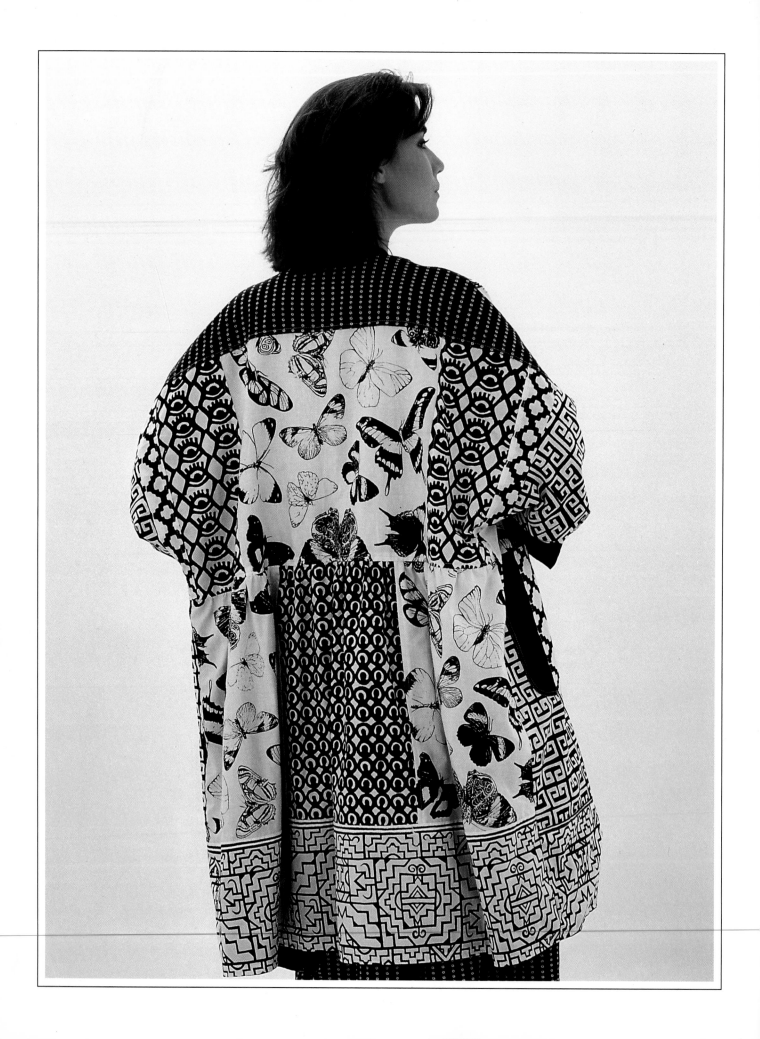

INTRODUCTION

It was in the Sixties when I was a student that I first became aware of screen printing. 'Pop art' was all the rage in America and screen printed images were being used by experimentalists as an integral part of their paintings. Two of my lecturers in graphics were experimenting with light-sensitive screens at the time and I remember taking home a poster that they had printed of Che Guevara and thinking that it was a miracle of modern technology.

Screen printing is basically a stencilling process - a craft of which the Japanese have been supreme masters for hundreds of years, creating amazingly intricate and beautiful designs with awesome skill. Originally, they worked with two identical waterproof stencils glued together, with a grid of human hair or strands of silk between them to stop the small pieces of the stencil moving about. Later, they developed a means of applying stencils to a fine silk mesh - a technique which became the foundation of modern screen printing.

Towards the end of the last century Japan was forced out of its long, self-imposed isolation, and the West was fascinated. Many of the Japanese arts and crafts were imported into America and Europe, and it was this contact which rekindled an interest in the old practice of stencilling. In 1907 a framed screen with a stencil attached was

(Opposite) This striking black and white ensemble shows how a number of designs can be successfully combined to create a truly unique fashion garment. The fabrics were printed with 'Key Design', 'Butterflies', 'Ndebele Border' and 'Ashanti Prints'. (Above) When you suddenly have nothing to wear, screen printing skills can be very useful. The versatile 'Butterflies' design was quickly printed and this youthful outfit made for an impromptu party - all in an afternoon.

first patented in England. The idea was quickly seized upon and soon exploited commercially for printing posters, displays and advertisements.

In the 1920s textile designers began to realize the potential of the method. Exclusive designs could be screen printed faster than block printed fabrics but in smaller quantities than those that were mass-produced. The same trend is noticeable today: many designers are having relatively small runs of material screen printed for unique ranges of clothes. (The minimum quantity specified by some professional screen printers is a hundred metres compared to orders of a few thousand required for printing by any other process.)

When I left university, I never in my wildest dreams thought that I would become a textile designer and printer. It was a development that just happened through a series of unconnected events. As I travelled through South America with my husband, I found myself fascinated by the colourful fabrics which were to be seen everywhere. I was especially drawn to the rural, even primitive places where people still live close to their traditional way of life and the crafts associated with it.

Our two-year sojourn in Peru afforded many opportunities to travel in that wonderful country. The museums abound in examples of woven materials, many over a thousand years old, the colours beautifully preserved by the dry air; and still today the tradition of weaving and dyeing is in evidence all over Peru.

Even the smallest of Peruvian villages has a weekly market where the 'campesinos' sell and barter anything from hand-woven ponchos and jerseys to corn and potatoes. On one occasion, travelling over the freezing cold and windswept Altiplano, we passed small groups of stone and adobe dwellings. Outside one was a woman, kneeling at her loom: four stakes driven into the ground, with the warp attached. Everything she knew had been passed down over the generations, not only the intricate patterns she wove, but also the method of shearing the alpacas, and the spinning and dyeing of the wool.

When my children became more independent, I enrolled in a one-year correspondence course in graphics. Towards the end of the year I had to experiment with a graphic medium of my choice. I chose screen printing and it has absorbed me compulsively ever since. I am continually experimenting with various techniques, and that alone can be very exciting. My real interest, however, lies in colour and design - for me, the techniques are the means to accomplishing my ideas.

To teach myself as much as possible about screen printing I read every book I could find on the subject, but the information was scattered and incomplete, and it was definitely not intended for domestic application. The professional screen printers I spoke to were very helpful, and the pamphlets from screen printing suppliers also provided me with invaluable details, but again, no source gave the whole story. So I had no choice but to piece the fragments together and experiment.

Since I took my first tentative steps there has been a surge of interest in screen printing as a home industry, yet still no book has emerged to guide newcomers to the craft. I therefore decided that it would be useful to collate all the information I have gathered over the years, both to help beginners over the first stumbling blocks and to show even experienced printers the vast potential of screen printing.

When people first start screen printing, the temptation is to begin with light-sensitive screens, because these are what the professionals all use and all the equipment is readily available. I would suggest, however, that those of you who are beginners start off with paper stencils, as described in chapter two. In this way you are not confused by too many new facts and procedures all at once. The only specialist items you will need are a screen, a squeegee and textile printing inks; everything else is normal household equipment.

After working through a few projects in the second chapter, try one or two projects from each of the other chapters, each of which deals with a different method of applying a design to a screen. That way you will probably find one technique that you enjoy most because it suits your personal method of working.

Once the basic techniques have been mastered, a whole new field of design and colour will open up before you. Search through your local library for books on the history of textiles. Study the designs of beautiful old Turkish silk velvets, Kashmir shawls, the painted and printed cottons of India, mediaeval tapestries, kelims and African textiles. Visit museums and see what designs you can find there. Some of my favourite block-printed textiles were designed by William Morris, the founder of the Arts and Crafts Movement in the late 19th century, whose aim it was to bring back hand-crafted articles into everyday living as an alternative to the soulless products of machinery. Most of all, I find myself drawn to tribal designs and colours. Whether from South America, Africa or Europe, from this century or a thousand years ago, they all share a common vitality of design and depth of colour.

When I first started screen printing I printed on paper and I never knew what to do with all the prints I produced. Printing onto fabric, on the other hand, has limitless possibilities. I have printed all the cushions, curtains and blinds for our holiday cottage, and each member of the family has a specially designed quilt. I also try to print and make all my own clothes. Now, however, I print more fabric than I can possibly use myself, so I sell it at the local craft market.

If you are keen, fabric printing is the sort of hobby that can easily be developed into a business as there will always be a market for exclusive fabrics. And besides selling the fabric, there is also the potential for designing and making up items such as clothing, bed linen, table linen and soft furnishings.

I have been exceptionally fortunate in my choice of craft because, apart from the opportunity to make money while still being at home for my family, I just love screen printing. For me, working with colours and fabric is so fascinating and satisfying that I can barely tear myself away from my workroom. I am constantly planning new projects, paging through magazines and books for new ideas, or devising new ways of overcoming design or printing problems. The creative challenge of screen printing seems never-ending.

In this book I have endeavoured to unravel the mysteries of screen printing and, through a number of projects for the home, to reveal a new world of exciting creativity that you, too, can enter and explore at whatever level you wish.

CHAPTER ONE

THE BASICS

Screen printing is a process which may suggest something complicated and difficult at first, but it is actually very easy once you make a start. The most versatile of all printing techniques - and the most widely used - it can apply any pattern to almost any surface: from bottles and circuit boards to wallpaper and textiles.

This book is specifically about textiles, and it will teach you how to design and print your own unique fabrics for curtains, clothes, cushions and quilts - in fact, anything you are able to make out of cloth.

In this chapter you are introduced to the fundamentals of fabric screen printing. You will learn how to use the basic equipment, mix colours, make a print, apply various techniques for printing squares, borders, T-shirts and all-over designs, as well as the many ways of achieving perfect registration when you are printing in several colours. Once these basics have been understood, you should have no difficulty in moving on to the projects in the following chapters and getting down to some serious screen printing.

As you will gather from this chapter, screen printing can be enjoyed on many different levels and thrilling results are achieved for very little capital outlay. If you get 'hooked', though, you may well wish to extend your range of equipment and materials, all of which you will find readily available to home crafters through local suppliers.

To make a start you will need: a screen, a squeegee, a flat surface to print on, textile printing inks and, of course, fabric.

(Opposite) Starting up in screen printing requires surprisingly little specialized material and equipment. The basics, clockwise from left, are: a squeegee, a screen, paint brushes, textile printing inks and a chalk line. Also included in the picture are two sets of colour swatches. (Above) At work with the basics.

THE SCREEN

This is a fine gauze or mesh of natural or man-made fibres stretched over a rectangular frame. The mesh used to be made of silk - hence the term 'silk screening', which is still in common use today.

I usually buy ready-made screens from the suppliers. The frames are of welded steel tubing and the meshes are even and taut - an essential feature for registering multicolour prints.

Mesh sizes range from very coarse (30) to ultra-fine (90) - the numbers indicate the number of threads per 2.5 cm [1 in]. The coarser the mesh the more easily it prints but then the outlines of curved designs lose their smooth flow and become 'stepped'. Finer meshes, on the other hand, print more slowly but with greater precision and maximum detail.

Screens are available in a variety of sizes but almost all of the projects in this book can be printed using one screen measuring 61 cm x 56 cm [24 in x 22 in], with a 43 mesh. The two exceptions are 'Rag Doll' on page 80 and 'Persian Flowers' T-shirt on page 75.

Although screens are relatively inexpensive to purchase, if you are on a tight budget, or you wish to involve children, it can be fun to make the screen.

MAKING A SCREEN

The frame: If you can saw a piece of wood and hammer in a nail, then you can make your own screen.

Although the outside measurements of the home-made screen will not be the same as those of the steel-framed screen, the printing area (inside frame measurements) will be identical, that is 56 cm x 51 cm [22 in x 20 in]. Working with 4.4 cm-wide x 1 cm-thick [1¾ in-wide x ⅜ in-thick] meranti cover strip, you will need for the short side:
Four lengths measuring 51 cm [20 in]
Two lengths measuring 59.8 cm [23½ in]
and for the long side:
Four lengths measuring 64.8 m [25½ in]
Two lengths measuring 56 cm [22 in]

To avoid difficult joints:
1. Each side of the frame is made up of a sandwich of three strips, which are first glued and nailed together. On two of the sides the middle piece of the sandwich is shorter than the outer pieces, and on the other two sides it is longer, so that, when joined, they provide a good substitute for a mortise and tenon joint.

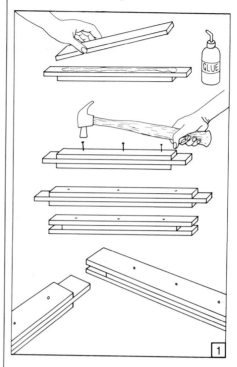

2. Glue the projecting pieces and fit them into the slots. Nail to secure them, making sure that the corners form precise right angles.
3. Sand the corners and edges with very coarse sandpaper to round them off so that they do not tear the mesh.

The mesh: I used to make my own screens with cotton organdie stretched on a wooden frame. They were very primitive, but for a beginner they are adequate. If you cannot find cotton organdie, polyester mesh is sold by the metre at screen printing suppliers. It is fairly expensive, but if cared for properly it will last many years.
1. Cut the mesh 10 cm [4 in] larger than the frame all round. (This is necessary in order to get a good grip on the mesh when stretching it.)
2. Secure one side of the mesh with a staple in the middle of one side of the frame. Pull the other side of the mesh as tightly as possible without tearing it and staple it to the opposite side.

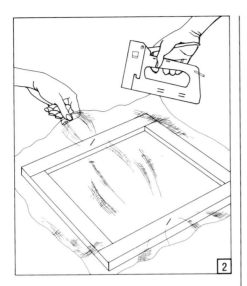

3. Now staple both sides of the mesh alternately, again keeping it as tight as possible. (You will need some help with this. Even so, there will still be a few wrinkles but these should disappear when the mesh is stretched in the opposite direction.)

4. Starting in the centre of the other two sides, staple the mesh in the same way.

5. Finish the screen by turning the excess mesh under and stapling it down.

THE SQUEEGEE

This is a length of stiff rubber or plastic, set into a handle and used to pull the ink over the surface of the mesh. It is the pressure that is applied to the squeegee that pushes the ink through the mesh and onto the fabric beneath.

A squeegee should measure about 6 cm [$2\frac{1}{2}$ in] shorter than the shortest inside measurement of your screen. For the screens used throughout this book a 46 cm-long [18 in-long] squeegee is ideal. It is possible to make your own squeegee, using the special rubber from a screen printing supplier and setting it in a piece of tongued-and-grooved pine. The woodwork teacher at my children's school made several this way for the 'Friendship Squares' project (see page 31). You could also use a window-washing squeegee sold at hardware shops if you only want to experiment, but the blade is too flexible for serious work.

THE PRINTING TABLE

Any flat surface can be used - as long as it does not wobble! The bigger it is the easier it is to print large pieces of fabric. A table tennis table can easily be converted into a temporary printing table by covering it with a thin piece of foam rubber and a sheet of vinyl. These can be removed after a printing session. However, some of the most innovative printing I have seen was done on a kitchen table with a blanket thrown over it.

If, however, you are going to do more than an occasional print, you will need a special table in order to work with long lengths of fabric - and also to avoid having to tidy up every evening. I made my own table from two sheets of chipboard joined end to end, strengthened with strips of pine and supported on four trestles. I spread an old carpet underfelt over the chipboard and covered it with a piece of smooth vinyl, securing both layers to the table top with staples.

To prevent fabric moving around while you print and then lifting up with the screen after printing, a special *pressure-sensitive adhesive*, available at screen printing suppliers, is spread over the vinyl with a piece of cardboard or a squeegee. It is important to spread only the thinnest layer of adhesive over the surface, otherwise the first piece of fabric to be printed will be very sticky. A *spray-on adhesive* (T-Fix) is a good temporary measure if a table is losing its stickiness.

> **— NOTE —**
> Keep the table covered with a sheet if it has adhesive on it, otherwise you will spend hours picking off bits of thread and fluff.

THE INKS

Textile printing inks are wonderful: they are odourless, water-soluble and non-toxic. They are 100% washable, too, provided they have been properly heat-set (see page 21). They can also be used for sponging and painting onto fabric, and are suitable for use in schools.

The term 'ink' is something of a misnomer, as the consistency is not that of a free-flowing liquid but of a paste, which is why a squeegee is required to spread it. It consists of an emulsion containing a binder and fixer to which pure pigments are added. There are two types of emulsion: one is transparent (referred to in this book as 'clear base') for printing onto light fabrics, the other is opaque for printing onto dark fabrics. You can either buy the pigment and base separately to mix yourself, or ready-mixed in the correct proportions by the suppliers.

To start with, it is cheaper to buy ready-mixed ink, as pure pigment is fairly expensive and only available in large quantities.

The trade name of the inks I use is Sericol. I am sure there are other very good inks on the market, but these are the only ones I use and I have always found them perfect for my needs as a home-based printer.

The success of screen printed fabric depends as much on the mixing of colours as on the design. You will find that suppliers carry a dazzling array of inks, but if you are just starting out it would be best to begin with four basic ready-to-use colours. These are *magenta, azure* and *primrose* (the purest primary colours in the Sericol range) and *black*. They are available in 1 kg [2 lb 2 oz] buckets and from them virtually any colour can be mixed. You will also need to buy a 5 kg [11 lb] bucket of *clear base* to lighten them as they are too dark to use neat.

Mixing Your Own Colours
From the three basic colours (magenta, azure and primrose) you will first need to mix three secondary and six tertiary colours in order to have in stock the 12 colours in the colour wheel. Using these, try a few exercises in colour mixing and make a set of colour swatches to help you in planning colours for future projects. You will need:

Textile inks
 – 1 litre [1¾ pints] primrose
 – 500 ml [17½ fl oz] magenta + 500 ml [17½ fl oz] clear base
 – 500 ml [17½ fl oz] azure + 500 ml [17½ fl oz] clear base
Sponges
 These are required to apply the different coloured inks to the sample squares: pieces of household foam sponge (about 8 cm x 5 cm [3 in x 2 in]) are ideal.
Fabric
 Cut out 60 x 20 cm [8 in] squares of

pure white cotton. (The inks are very transparent and even a cream-coloured calico will affect the final colour [see 'Printing coloured fabrics' on page 16].
Containers
 Set aside 12 x 500 ml [17½ fl oz] jars, with lids, in which to mix your ink. (For the later mixing exercises you will need a selection of smaller containers.)

THE METHOD
When measuring out your inks, it is not critical to measure precisely to the last drop, but it is important to be consistent, so that when you need to remix a colour it will be the same. Stir the inks together thoroughly until there are no streaks. Then, once you have mixed a colour, label it. It is very frustrating if you cannot find a colour and have to re-test them all in order to find the right one.

To make *primary, secondary* and *tertiary colours* mix the following:

1. *Yellow* - put 400 ml [14 fl oz] primrose into a small container.
2. *Lime-green* - mix 300 ml [10½ fl oz] primrose with 100 ml [3½ fl oz] azure.
3. *Green* - mix 200 ml [7 fl oz] primrose with 200 ml [7 fl oz] azure.
4. *Emerald green* - mix 100 ml [3½ fl oz] primrose with 300 ml [10½ fl oz] azure.
5. *Turquoise* - put 400 ml [14 fl oz] azure into a small container.
6. *Royal blue* - mix 300 ml [10½ fl oz] azure with 100 ml [3½ fl oz] magenta.
7. *Navy blue* - mix 200 ml [7 fl oz] azure with 200 ml [7 fl oz] magenta.
8. *Purple* - mix 100 ml [3½ fl oz] azure with 300 ml [10½ fl oz] magenta.
9. *Magenta* - put 400 ml [14 fl oz] magenta into a small container.
10. *Scarlet* - mix 300 ml [10½ fl oz] magenta with 100 ml [3½ fl oz] primrose.
11. *Orange* - mix 200 ml [7 fl oz] magenta with 200 ml [7 fl oz] primrose.
12. *Yellow-orange* - mix 100 ml [3½ fl oz] magenta with 300 ml [10½ fl oz] primrose.

Take 12 squares of cotton fabric and sponge on each of the 12 colours. (Just dip a piece of sponge into a colour and wipe it over the square, then smooth it

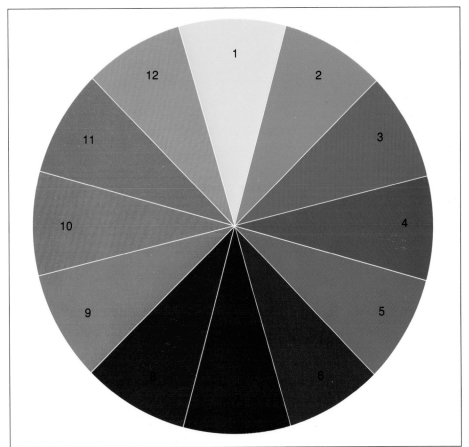

The colour wheel is
an indispensable
aid to colour
mixing. From these
12 colours any
shade can be
mixed.

with the sponge until it is even and there are no ridges of ink on the surface.) When the colours are dry, iron to set them, then write the formula for each colour on the back of the relevant square and number the squares from 1 to 12. From these 12 colours an incredible range can be mixed.

JEWEL COLOURS

When I am mixing a colour and it looks too bright, I always add to it a little of the colour that appears opposite it on the colour wheel - its *complementary colour.* For example, if a turquoise (no. 5) looks too intense, I add a tiny quantity of orange (no. 11). The colour becomes less bright and more subtle, but it still remains distinctly turquoise. Similarly, a magenta (no. 9) that is too garish mellows with the addition of a small amount of green (no. 3).

Try the exercise below to see what happens to colours when a little of a colour's complement is added.

1. Mix 30 ml [2 tbsp] of colour no. 1 (yellow) with 2.5 ml [$\frac{1}{2}$ tsp] of colour no. 7 (navy blue).
2. Mix 30 ml [2 tbsp] of colour no. 2 with 2.5 ml [$\frac{1}{2}$ tsp] of colour no. 8.
3. Mix 30 ml [2 tbsp] of colour no. 3 with 2.5 ml [$\frac{1}{2}$ tsp] of colour no. 9.
4. Mix 30 ml [2 tbsp] of colour no. 4 with 2.5 ml [$\frac{1}{2}$ tsp] of colour no. 10.
5. Mix 30 ml [2 tbsp] of colour no. 5 with 2.5 ml [$\frac{1}{2}$ tsp] of colour no. 11.
6. Mix 30 ml [2 tbsp] of colour no. 6 with 2.5 ml [$\frac{1}{2}$ tsp] of colour no. 12.
7. Mix 30 ml [2 tbsp] of colour no. 7 with 2.5 ml [$\frac{1}{2}$ tsp] of colour no. 1.
8. Mix 30 ml [2 tbsp] of colour no. 8 with 2.5 ml [$\frac{1}{2}$ tsp] of colour no. 2.
9. Mix 30 ml [2 tbsp] of colour no. 9 with 2.5 ml [$\frac{1}{2}$ tsp] of colour no. 3.
10. Mix 30 ml [2 tbsp] of colour no. 10 with 2.5 ml [$\frac{1}{2}$ tsp] of colour no. 4.
11. Mix 30 ml [2 tbsp] of colour no. 11 with 2.5 ml [$\frac{1}{2}$ tsp] of colour no. 5.
12. Mix 30 ml [2 tbsp] of colour no. 12 with 2.5 ml [$\frac{1}{2}$ tsp] of colour no. 6.

Sponge the colours onto 12 more cotton squares. When the colours are dry, iron to set them, then write the formula on the back of each and number them from 13 to 24.

DULLER COLOURS

To obtain slightly duller colours, mix 30 ml [2 tbsp] of a colour with 5 ml [1 tsp] of its complementary colour. For example, mix 30 ml [2 tbsp] of colour no. 1 (yellow) with 5 ml [1 tsp] of colour no. 7 (navy blue). Remember to write the formula on the back of each square and number them from 25 to 36.

PASTELS

To each of the 12 colours of the colour wheel add four parts of clear base to give you colours 37 to 48. Then add four parts of clear base to one part of each of the jewel colours to obtain soft and different pastels (colours 49 to 60).

You now have your 12 main colours from which you have mixed a further 48. If you like earthy colours, try adding more of each colour's complement. If you enjoy working with pastels, try adding varying amounts of clear base to all the colour wheel, jewel and duller colours. The possibilities are endless.

Always write the formula on the back of the swatch you have created so that you will be able to remix the colour.

> **—— NOTE ——**
> Mixing colours takes a long time - sometimes as long as printing them - but the success of a printed design ultimately rests with the colours. It is critical, therefore, that you get them right. Take the time not just to add a little of this and a little of that, but to try the colours on the fabric you will be using and observe how they react to different kinds of light. You will never be sorry that you took that time - but you might be sorry that you did not.

> **—— HINT ——**
> Any colour must be dry before it can be judged properly. The inks dry much lighter than they appear when wet. A hair dryer is useful to speed up the drying process.

PRINTING COLOURED FABRICS

Printing inks are transparent, so if yellow is printed onto blue fabric it will become green, or if maroon is printed onto yellow fabric it will look brown. If a transparent ink is printed onto black it will not show at all. So when you want to print a light design onto a dark fabric you will need to buy opaque inks.

The only project in this book that uses opaque inks is the 'Persian Flowers' T-shirt on page 76.

THE FABRICS

Textile printing inks are effective on natural and man-made fibres but I always prefer printing onto 100% cotton. This, however, is a purely personal preference.

If you are printing onto calico, be sure that it is pure cotton as some makes of calico are at least 50% synthetic. To test for synthetic (polyester) content, burn a little piece of fabric. Cotton burns slowly and leaves a fine ash, while polyester burns fast, gives off a chemical smell and leaves a hard, black plastic residue.

Although cotton knits are difficult to spread on the printing table, they print well, absorbing any excess ink which, on other fabrics, would remain on the surface and result in an uneven print. When made up they drape particularly well.

> **—— NOTE ——**
> Avoid all cottons with crease-resistant, glazed or satin finishes. Although textile ink will adhere to a fabric finish, it will wash out eventually because it has not been absorbed by the cotton.

PREPARING THE FABRIC

Cotton fabric is available which has been prepared for printing or dyeing. This is so useful as washing and ironing long pieces of fabric is tedious.

If the cotton fabric that you have bought is not labelled 'prepared for dyeing', it must first be washed in cold water to remove the starch and then in hot water (above 60 °C) to shrink it. Using a washing machine, wash the fabric twice on a cold cycle and then, with detergent and fabric softener, on a hot cycle.

To remove all the creases from pure cotton, always iron the fabric when it is damp. Cotton knit, on the other hand, does not need ironing.

Spread the fabric on the printing table and smooth it out with the palm of your hand, making sure that the warp and weft of the fabric lie at right angles to each other.

While smoothing out the fabric, feel for any foreign objects underneath the cloth that could cause printing irregularities or damage to your screen. Even if you have just got everything straight, lift it up again to remove even the slightest lump or ridge which you have missed.

> **—— NOTE ——**
> The surface facing the inside of a roll of fabric is the correct side to print on.

REGISTRATION

This is the method of putting the screen down in exactly the right place on the fabric. For a long time I judged the position by peering through the mesh, and it works quite well until the screen becomes darkened by the ink. I now find it better to mark out the fabric with a chalk line.

CHALK LINE
Obtainable fairly cheaply at any hardware store, this item comprises a small plastic case, inside which is rolled a length of string. Powdered blue chalk is emptied into the case through a small sliding aperture; the case is then shaken to impregnate the string with chalk, after which the string is pulled out and placed along the fabric on the printing table. Stretching the string tight, a finger is placed firmly on each end, while a third hand is enlisted to pluck the string up at a more or less central point. When released with a snap, the string deposits a neat, very straight line on the fabric.

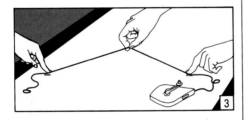

FABRIC MARKING PEN
This is a fibre-tip pen that marks with a purple or turquoise line. It can be bought at a shop that sells sewing requirements. The purple line disappears after a day, depending on the humidity, while the turquoise line can be removed from the fabric by wiping with a damp cloth, or washing.

A Border
METHOD 1
This is a very easy method (used for 'Peruvian Braids' [see page 24]).

1. Mark a chalk line along the length of the fabric where the lower edge of the design will be printed.
2. Lower the screen into its first printing

position on the left-hand side of the fabric (it is possible to see through the mesh to position it correctly on the chalk line) and mark the frame of the screen at the two points where it crosses the line.
3. To position the screen correctly for subsequent prints, look through the mesh until you can see the right-hand side of the previous print, and put the screen down so that there is a 2 mm [$\frac{1}{12}$ in] overlap. Check that the marks on the frame are touching the chalk line as this keeps the border straight, then print.

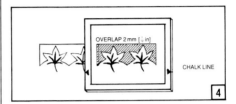

OVERLAP 2 mm [$\frac{1}{12}$ in]   CHALK LINE

> **HINT**
> When registering a border or an all-over design it is necessary to mark the frame of the screen. To avoid the build-up of a confusing array of marks, stick masking tape onto the frame and make your marks on the tape. It is easily removed at the end of the printing project, together with all the marks.

METHOD 2
For this second method (used for the green 'Hawaiian Quilt' border [see page 27]) you will need a straight piece of wood the length of your printing table. (It is easy to print a border if you have a long straight edge against which to butt the lower edge of the screen.) Use clamps to secure it to the table. A chalk line is not necessary with this method as the wood keeps the screen, and consequently the border, straight.
1. Place the screen on the left-hand side of the fabric and measure the width of the *design*. Then, using a fabric marking pen, and starting from the extreme right-hand edge of the *screen*, mark off the width of the design along the entire length of the fabric.

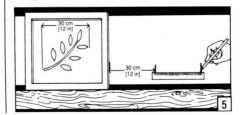

30 cm [12 in]   30 cm [12 in]

2. After making the first print, move the screen so that the first mark on the fabric lines up with the outer right-hand edge of the screen. This means that each section is printed with the screen touching the wood at the bottom, as well as one of the marks on the fabric on the right-hand edge of the screen.

A BORDER REPEATED TO CREATE AN
ALL-OVER DESIGN
Using the first method of registration with the chalk line, the border can be repeated close together to create an all-over design.

An All-over Design

Every design has two dimensions - width and height. Mark off one of these dimensions along both selvedges of the fabric and the other along both cut ends, then join the opposite marks by means of chalk lines to form a grid over the fabric.

Initially it will be possible to print the material by simply looking at the chalk lines through the mesh, but after many prints - particularly when printing in black - the build-up of ink will make it increasingly difficult to see clearly.

Before starting to print, therefore, place the screen on the fabric and line up a square with the design on the screen. The chalk lines will intersect each side of the frame in two places. Mark these eight points clearly on the frame. Now the screen can be put down accurately in any square just by lining up the marks on the outside of the frame with the chalk lines.

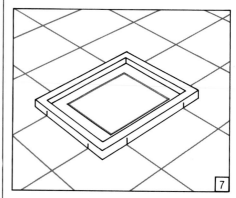

Multicolour Printing

This applies mainly to film-cut stencils and light-sensitive emulsion stencils which are explained in detail in chapters four and five. Before elaborating on the various methods, however, I must say that, due to my limited facilities, I try to avoid multicolour printing as much as possible because in most instances it requires the preparation of as many screens as there are colours to be printed.

I like to print in one colour and paint or sponge on additional colours (see pages 25 and 53). The result is most effective and I suggest that you try this method first before becoming involved in the technicalities of perfect registration.

Nevertheless, there are several methods of registration for multicolour printing suitable for the home-based printer.

METHOD 1
The easiest way to manage multicolour printing is to have a thick black outline that is printed first (see the squares printed for 'Ndebele Quilt' on page 54). Then, by looking through the screen at the first print, the next colours can easily be lined up. There can be a good overlap, too, because any transparent ink printed onto black cannot be seen.

METHOD 2
Using any one of the above-mentioned systems for registering a design, print the darkest colour of the design first (such as the black outline of 'Poppies' on page 72). Then, using the same registration system, print the subsequent colours,

making the final adjustments to the screen by lining it up with the design already printed.

This system is fairly time-consuming and is not always completely accurate, but it is easy and works well enough. *It is important not to move the fabric between prints if the position of the second and subsequent prints is critical.*

METHOD 3

If you want to print a design onto a set of panels which are smaller than your screen (in screen printing terminology a 'panel' is anything that is not a length of fabric):

1. Place the first panel to be printed on the printing table, smoothing it out firmly so that it is held in place by the pressure-sensitive adhesive; then stick masking tape on the table to mark the *outsides* of the corners of the *panel*.

2. Lower the screen over the panel and when it is correctly positioned, stick masking tape on the printing table to mark the *exact* position of the four corners of the *screen*.

3. Print the panel in the first colour.

4. Lift the screen, remove the printed panel and put the next one in place, using the masking tape as a guide.

5. Now place the screen in its marked position and print again.

6. When all the printing in one colour has been completed, the screens for the next colours can use the same marks, making it easy to register all the colours, especially if the screens themselves have been registered.

METHOD 4

If you do not have a big table and want to register screens for multicolour printing, the screen can be attached to a small table or piece of hardboard with a pair of hinges. (Special hinges are available from screen printing suppliers.) This way the screen remains in the same place and the fabric is placed underneath it on a pre-determined mark.

1. Have several pieces of hardboard cut to the same size as your screen and coat them with a pressure-sensitive adhesive (see page 13).

2. Press each item to be printed onto a board to keep the fabric stable in be-

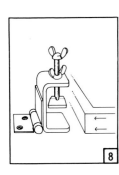

tween printing each colour, and place the first one under the raised screen.

3. Line up the fabric with the screen, then mark its precise position on the table with masking tape.

4. Next, lower the screen onto the fabric and print the design.

5. Raise the screen and remove the fabric and board.

6. When all the designs have been printed in the first colour (having made sure that each board has been placed in the correct position on the masking tape) remove the screen and clean it.

7. Now place the screen for the second colour in the hinges. Before clamping it, however, lower it over one of the first prints (which you have already correctly positioned on the masking tape marks) in order to make quite sure that both the screen and the area to be printed line up precisely. When the screen is correctly positioned over the print, clamp the hinges and print the design as before.

This is an excellent system if you have limited space as the boards provide you with a portable printing surface that can easily be stacked away. It is ideal for printing small items, such as labels, place mats, cushion covers or T-shirts.

METHOD 5

When printing more than one colour onto a T-shirt or panel:

1. Attach a long strip of angle iron to the printing table by means of clamps. Then, at regular intervals, clamp small steel brackets at right angles to it.

2. To the right of each bracket spread a T-shirt (with a piece of adhesive-sprayed hardboard inside to separate the front from the back) or a panel.

3. Lower the screen over the first T-shirt/panel so that the lower edge of the frame touches the angle iron and the lower left-hand corner presses up against a bracket, then print the first colour.

4. When each item in the row has been printed with the first colour, put the screen to one side and lower the next screen for the second colour over the first T-shirt/panel. Once again, the lower edge of the frame must touch the angle iron, while the lower left-hand corner presses against a bracket.

5. Repeat this process with all the colours, then remove the T-shirts/panels from the table and hang them up to dry.

6. Set out the next row and start printing with the first colour again.

> **—— NOTE ——**
>
> When using this system of registration for multicolour printing, it is important that the design is in exactly the same place on each screen (see the 'Persian Flowers' T-shirt on page 76).
>
> It is also important to ensure that the ink does not dry on the screens while printing the other colours as dried ink is extremely difficult to clean off (see page 20). After printing a colour onto the last T-shirt/panel in each set, lift the screen off and pull ink over the mesh with a squeegee, leaving a 3 mm [⅛ in] or so layer of ink. This will prevent the ink on the screen from drying out and clogging the mesh.

As you now have a variety of registration methods for printing designs onto fabric, as well as for multicolour printing, I suggest that you experiment with a few to determine which one suits you best.

PRINTING

Before starting to print:

1. Have a damp cloth ready for wiping your hands. Inky fingers invariably leave smudges on the fabric.

2. Decide where to rest your squeegee in between prints. If you leave it in the screen it always slides into the ink. (It is not necessary to wipe the ink off each time as it does not drip.)

3. Have a pile of newspapers cut and ready to place on wet ink. Alternatively, have a hair dryer to hand.

To print:

1. Place the screen in its first position for printing and spoon out the ink across the far side of the screen. For a 61 cm x 56 cm [24 in x 22 in] frame, 60 ml [4 tbsp] should be enough. Do not skimp because any excess can be returned to the jar afterwards.

2. Hold the squeegee firmly in both hands. If you are a beginner, it is better to have someone hold the screen down while you are printing as it may move and smudge the print. Place the squeegee on the far side of the ink and, holding it at an angle of 45°, pull the ink gently over the mesh towards you. (See diagram 27 on page 37.)

3. Return the squeegee to the far side of the screen and repeat the process, this time pressing more firmly to remove all excess ink and to ensure that the ink is evenly distributed.

> **—— NOTE ——**
>
> The number of times you pull the squeegee over the mesh depends on the coarseness of the mesh, the fabric being printed, the consistency of the ink and the hardness of the squeegee rubber. Therefore, before printing on the main fabric, several test prints should be made to establish how many pulls will be necessary.

4. When you are satisfied with the distribution of ink, place your squeegee in a safe, stable place and carefully lift the screen off the fabric.

> **—— NOTE ——**
>
> It is best to lift the screen as if you were turning the page of a book. In other words, keeping the left-hand side of the screen pressed down on the fabric, gently lift the right-hand side of the screen until it loses contact with the fabric. If the screen is lifted off as if you were removing a plate from a table, it will draw the fabric off the adhesive surface. Apart from having to smooth out the fabric again, this might result in a smudged print.

CLEANING THE SCREEN

A screen should last you for many years, so take special care of it. *Never* let textile printing ink dry on your mesh as it is very difficult to remove. If you have to leave the screen for a few minutes during printing, either pull a fresh layer of ink over the surface or leave the screen on top of the last print made. The moisture of the ink on the fabric will keep the screen damp for about 10 minutes. Flooding the screen with ink will keep it moist for about 30 minutes, depending on the ambient temperature.

As soon as the printing has been completed, hose the screen down using maximum water pressure in order to remove every last trace of ink from the mesh. If the screen does get a little clogged, take it to either the screen printing supply shop or a garage workshop where it can be sprayed with a high pressure hose. Alternatively, using a stiff brush with a handle, apply a mixture of strong *ink solvent* (Autosolve) and *cleaning paste* (Autopaste) to the screen. Leave it for a few minutes, then hose off. (These are very strong chemicals and give off a horrible smell, so it is advisable to wear a mask and gloves when using them and to work outside.)

The methods for removing 'fixed' stencils from the mesh are explained in later chapters.

HEAT-SETTING

To make printed fabric colour-fast it is necessary to subject it to a high temperature. This process is called heat-setting.

Because I sell most of the fabric I print, I like to have it professionally heat-set. (The curing time in a professional oven is three minutes at 150-170 °C [300-340 °F] and the charge is relatively small.) Look up 'screen printers' or 'silk screen printers' in the Yellow Pages (Classified Directory) and phone a few to find out if they heat-set or 'cure' other people's fabric. If you draw a blank there, find a professional laundry that has large metal rolling irons at least 150 cm [6 ft] wide for pressing sheets. If the fabric is put through these twice, it should be fine.

For smaller pieces, you may prefer to do the heat-setting at home. Occasionally I have used my tumble dryer, putting in about two metres at a time and leaving it on the hottest setting for half an hour. (If you use this method, first make sure that the ink is completely dry, otherwise it will smudge.)

It is also possible to use a domestic pressing machine to heat-set fabric, but care must be taken to ensure that every single square centimetre receives an equal amount of heat. The same applies to any heat-setting done with an iron. (The iron must be turned to the setting for cotton, ie hot.)

PARTIAL HEAT-SETTING
When additional colour is to be sponged or brushed onto printed fabric it is essen-

> **NOTE**
> The colours really do hold fast if properly heat-set. I make virtually all my clothes from my own printed fabrics. Most of them are washed in the washing machine and none of the designs has run or faded.

tial that the ink is partially heat-set, or at least *thoroughly* dry, otherwise the design will smudge. Either hang the freshly printed fabric in the sun or, when the ink is dry to the touch, put it in the tumble drier for 15 to 20 minutes or iron it. If none of these methods is possible, hang the fabric up indoors and leave it for one to two days, or longer, depending on the ambient temperature and humidity.

OTHER BASIC EQUIPMENT

Craft knife - ideal for cutting out paper stencils.

Cutting board - essential for resting paper stencils on when cutting them out with a craft knife. (A piece of hardboard serves this purpose well but a wad of newspapers can be used instead.)

Packaging tape - used to reduce the size of the printing area of the screen and as a 'resting place' for the ink before and after it has been pulled across the screen. (This tape is 48 mm [2 in] wide and is a brown, extra sticky type of Sellotape. It is not to be confused with rolls of gummed brown paper.)

Soft lead (HB) pencil - used for marking the mesh. (A hard lead will damage your mesh.)

Ruler and/or tape measure.

Set square.

All-purpose scissors.

Paint brushes (2.5 cm [1 in] wide), as used in home decorating, with the length of the bristles shortened by half to create firm, stubby applicators. These are used for applying textile inks to narrow areas of printed fabric.

Water colour brush - a sable or imitation sable brush (size 3) for design work on the screen or on tracing paper.

• When directions refer to 'the squeegee side' of the screen, it means the 'hollow' side on which the ink is placed and where the printing is done.

• When 'the underside' of the screen is referred to, it is the side on which the mesh is stretched over the frame and which is placed on the fabric when printing. When the underside is facing up, the screen is said to be 'upside down'.

CHAPTER TWO

PAPER STENCILS

When I started screen printing at home I first used hand-cut film stencils, and later moved on to light-sensitive stencils. It was only much later that I realised that to print fairly simple shapes paper stencils could be used. Once I began thinking of designs especially for paper stencils I suddenly found screen printing even more exciting because it became more versatile - and definitely cheaper.

Paper stencils are so quick and easy to work with. They do not require any finnicky or time-consuming process to adhere them to the screen. They simply stick themselves to the mesh as soon as they come into contact with the printing ink.

Because the cost of a stencil cut from brown wrapping paper is negligible, a design can be cut for the single printing of a unique T-shirt or a test design and then discarded. This would not be cost-effective with hand-cut film or light-sensitive stencils. At the same time, many metres of fabric can be printed from one piece of paper before it needs to be replaced. There is also the advantage that if a design does not work, the stencil can be thrown away without a moment's hesitation.

The paper stencil should never be scorned - the cut or torn edge of a piece of paper has a character all of its own and I have seen some wonderful fabric designs printed from paper. Compare the simple designs created by the early American settlers with the high level of sophistication achieved by the Japanese and you will have some idea of the incredible scope of paper.

Basic materials: screen (61 cm x 56 cm [24 in x 22 in]); squeegee (46 cm [18 in] long); textile printing inks (magenta, azure, primrose, black and clear base); tracing paper; HB pencil; ruler; brown wrapping paper; cutting board; craft knife; scissors; packaging tape; chalk line; fabric marking pen.

(Opposite) An astonishing variety of designs and level of complexity can be achieved using paper and scissors, as can be seen from the work of 12-year-olds in this 'Friendship Quilt'.
(Above) 'Peruvian Braids' spring to life when sponged with vibrant colours.

PERUVIAN BRAIDS

Every village market in Peru has an endless array of woven braids to sell, and the designs are wonderful. Llamas, cats, birds and frogs abound, as well as an amazing variety of abstract designs. Braids printed with ethnic designs can be just as stunning and are so simple to make. Use them as trimmings for clothes, bags, towels and cushions either in a single colour on white, or colourwashed afterwards with textile inks, or embroidered and beaded for added textural interest.

The idea for the frog design came from a Peruvian stone carving and the cat design from an ancient woven cloth.

Additional Materials

2 paint brushes: 2.5 cm [1 in] wide (bristle length halved)
Pieces of soft foam sponge
Suggested fabric: calico or medium-weight cotton
Designs: (1) and (2) on pages 82 and 83

Test Print

If you have printed before there is no need to do this test print.

1. Trace one frog onto a piece of brown paper.
2. Resting the tracing on your cutting board, cut out the frog and its eyes with your craft knife. Place the frog on a small piece of cotton calico.
3. Take a piece of brown paper the same size as your screen and in the centre cut a rectangle slightly larger than the frog. Discard the paper rectangle and place the brown paper frame over the frog.

4. Place the screen, squeegee-side up, on top of the paper frame and frog stencil.
5. Spoon some black ink onto the mesh of the screen that is lying over the brown paper frame and, with someone else holding the screen down so that it does not move, pull the ink towards you with the squeegee. Then, exerting a little more pressure on the mesh, pull the ink over the surface of the screen twice more to ensure a good even print.
6. Carefully lift the screen off and inspect your print. The paper will have stuck to your screen, so you can make a few more prints if you want to.
7. Peel off the paper frame and frog stencil and wash your screen with a strong jet of water.

These test pieces need not be wasted; they can be sewn onto the front of a T-shirt or made into a pocket or patch.

The Stencil

Trace design (1) onto a piece of brown paper and neatly cut out the row of four frogs with a craft knife. You are going to use both the cut-out frogs (the positive shape) and the background paper (the negative shape) for printing.

The Screen

1. Using an HB pencil, draw a 12 cm x 24 cm [$4\frac{3}{4}$ in x $9\frac{1}{2}$ in] rectangle in the centre of the underside of the screen.
2. Cover the mesh, except the marked out rectangle, with packaging tape.

The Fabric

1. Cut or rip the fabric into an 18 cm-wide [7 in-wide] strip, from selvedge to selvedge, or down the length of the fabric.
2. Lay the fabric strip down on the printing table, smoothing it lightly with your hand to remove the wrinkles, and then pressing it onto the adhesive. Make sure there are no threads or bumps behind the fabric (see page 16).

Registration

1. Snap the chalk line (see page 17) 3 cm [$1\frac{1}{4}$ in] up from the lower edge of the strip.
2. Take your fabric marking pen and, using the chalk line as the base, draw a 12 cm x 24 cm [$4\frac{3}{4}$ in x $9\frac{1}{2}$ in] rectangle on the left-hand side of the fabric strip.

> **— NOTE —**
> Always overlap the strips of packaging tape so that no ink can ooze between them when printing.

3. Position the 'negative' frog stencil, complete with eyes (cut from the 'positive' frogs), just above the chalk line. Above these, position the cut-out 'positive' frogs so that they face in the opposite direction to the stencil frogs.

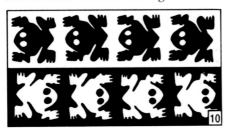

4. Lower the screen over the paper stencils so that you can see the frogs through the mesh in the rectangle that you have taped off.

5. Mark the two places on your screen where the chalk line intersects the frame (see diagram 7 on page 18). These will help you register your screen on subsequent prints when the screen gets a bit messy and it becomes difficult to see the chalk line through the mesh.

Printing

1. Spoon black ink onto the mesh at the top of the screen. Using the squeegee, pull the ink gently over the surface, so that a thin layer is spread evenly over the mesh. Pull the ink firmly over the surface twice more, holding the frame down with one hand so that it does not move.

2. Remove the squeegee and put it somewhere safe. Then lift up the screen to look at your print.

3. Dry the right-hand side of the print for a couple of minutes with a hair dryer, just until the shine has gone from the surface of the ink.

4. Put the screen down on the fabric so that you can see 2 mm [$\frac{1}{12}$ in] of the first print on the left-hand side of the printing aperture in the screen (see diagram 4 on page 17). Ensure that the two marks on the frame line up with the chalk line. You are now ready to print again. Continue printing in this way to the end of the fabric.

Finishing

Put the printed fabric in the tumble-dryer for 30 minutes on the highest setting, or iron it, to heat-set the ink. If you intend brushing on additional colour, however, only partial heat-setting is necessary (see page 21).

APPLYING ADDITIONAL COLOUR

1. Return the fabric strip to the printing table and smooth it out in readiness for the colours to be painted on.

2. For bright, primitive colours, try using complementary colours, such as emerald green (no. 4 on the colour wheel on page 15) and scarlet (no. 10). Equal quantities of clear base must be added to lighten the colours, otherwise the printed design will not be seen. Finally, to make the colours easier to apply with a brush, add about 25% water to each colour. Suggested quantities:

For the *emerald green*, mix 75 ml [$2\frac{1}{2}$ fl oz] azure with 25 ml [5 tsp] primrose. Add 100 ml [$3\frac{1}{2}$ fl oz] clear base and stir well. Dilute with 50 ml [10 tsp] water.

For the *scarlet,* mix 75 ml [$2\frac{1}{2}$ fl oz] magenta with 25 ml [5 tsp] primrose. Add 100 ml [$3\frac{1}{2}$ fl oz] clear base and stir well. Dilute with 50 ml [10 tsp] water.

3. Using a clean 2.5 cm [1 in] paint brush for each colour, paint the emerald green fairly thickly onto one stripe of frogs. Smooth away any excess ink with a sponge. Then paint the scarlet onto the other stripe. (It is best to use a different sponge for each colour.)

4. Leave the fabric to dry, then heat-set.

> **— NOTE —**
> The cat design (2) is printed in exactly the same way.

Brushing on colour is literally child's play: it is easy, fun and instantly rewarding.

HAWAIIAN QUILT

There are two features which distinguish real Hawaiian quilts: only one decorative design is cut to cover the entire quilt, and that design - which is appliquéd on - is always based on some natural, organic form. In this project I have used the same idea but on a smaller scale, cutting organic forms from folded pieces of paper and repeating them to fill the quilt.

As a wonderful family holiday project, an album quilt could be made by cutting out as many patterns as the children can think of and printing them either in one colour or in many wonderful wild colours. The resulting quilt would be a real family heirloom with memories of happy times all working together.

Additional Materials
Narrow plank of wood
Set square
Sheet of thin card
Fabric (to make a 230 cm x 180 cm [$90\frac{1}{2}$ in x 71 in] double bed quilt):
  For the squares, backing and trim: –
  9 m x 150 cm-wide [10 yds x 59 in-wide] calico, or 10.5 m x 120 cm-wide [$11\frac{1}{2}$ yds x 48 in-wide] calico
  Batting (wadding) – 240 cm x 190 cm [$94\frac{1}{2}$ in x $74\frac{3}{4}$ in]
Designs: (3), (4) and (5) on pages 82 and 83

THE SQUARES

The Stencils
1. Cut a 40 cm [$15\frac{3}{4}$ in] square from brown paper. Fold it as if you were going to cut out a snowflake pattern.

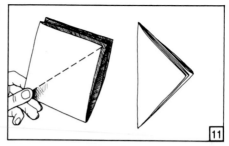

2. Draw a design of your own onto the paper, or trace design (3) from the book.

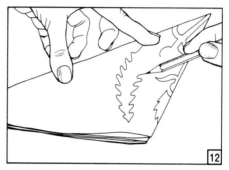

3. Holding the folds firmly together with one hand so that they do not slip, carefully cut around the pencil lines. Keep the little pieces that you cut out as they will be used later for the borders.

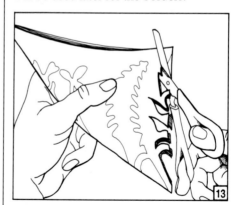

4. Now unfold the paper.
5. Cut another 40 cm [$15\frac{3}{4}$ in] square of brown paper and repeat this procedure with design (4).

The Screen
1. Stick packaging tape around the outside edges of the screen, leaving a 40 cm [$15\frac{3}{4}$ in] printing aperture.
2. Centre the pattern on the underside of the taped screen and secure it with tape all round the outside of the stencil so that the ink does not leak through.

The Colours

1. For the *pink*, mix 250 ml [9 fl oz] clear base with 15 ml [1 tbsp] magenta, 2.5 ml [$\frac{1}{2}$ tsp] azure and 1 ml [$\frac{1}{4}$ tsp] primrose.

2. Stir well and test the colour on a piece of the same fabric you are going to print onto. Dry it with a hair dryer and adjust the colour if necessary.

3. For the *green,* mix 250 ml [9 fl oz] clear base with 15 ml [1 tbsp] azure, 15 ml [1 tbsp] primrose and 2.5 ml [$\frac{1}{2}$ tsp] magenta.

4. Stir well and test as before.

The Fabric

Cut out 32 pieces of fabric, each measuring 35 cm [14 in] square. You will need 12 for printing in pink and 20 for printing in green.

Printing

THE PINK SQUARES

1. As it is not necessary to use registration marks when printing onto individual squares, simply lay out as many as you can on the printing table, far enough away from one another so that the screen does not touch an adjacent square.

2. Centre the screen over a square, then lower it into position. Spoon the pink ink onto the mesh and print.

3. As the squares are printed, hang them up to dry and spread out new squares.

4. When all 12 pink squares have been printed, remove the stencil (but not the border of packaging tape) and clean the screen by forcing a strong jet of water through the mesh. Scrub the mesh with a little non-abrasive household cleaner to

remove any stubborn ink, then rinse well.

5. Wipe the screen with a clean rag to remove the excess water and leave it to dry. (Do not leave the screen in the sun.)

THE GREEN SQUARES

1. Take the second stencil and stick it to the screen with packaging tape.

2. Lay out the remaining 20 squares and print in green.

3. Remove the stencil and all the packaging tape from the screen. Clean the screen and leave it to dry.

THE BORDERS

As can be seen in Persian carpets, borders are necessary to outline and complement the central design. In this project there are two borders, one in pink and one in green. To print them, a new method of registering a border is introduced, although you can use Method 1 for registering a border on page 17.

The Green Border

THE FABRIC

1. Cut or rip two strips measuring 150 cm x 15 cm [59 in x 6 in] and two more measuring 212 cm x 15 cm [83$\frac{1}{2}$ in x 6 in].

2. Place a long plank of wood on the printing table and clamp it to prevent it moving. (Bricks can be used to anchor the wood if you do not have any clamps.)

3. Spread and smooth out the strips of fabric on the printing table 14 cm [5$\frac{3}{4}$ in] away from the wood.

Unfolded, a simple paper pattern becomes an intricate design

The paper cut-outs which fell from the pattern are effectively put to use to make a complementary border.

THE STENCIL

1. On the left-hand side of the fabric, arrange four of the paper cut-outs which fell from the square stencils. Then, using a fabric marking pen, rule a line below and above the cut-outs parallel to the edge of the fabric. These lines should be 10 cm [4 in] apart and equidistant from the top and bottom edges of the material.

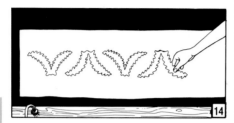

2. Now cut one of the cut-outs in half, vertically, and place one half at each end of the row. Check that all the shapes are equidistant.

3. With a set square, draw the exact ends of the stencil design at right angles to the wood to make a complete rectangle. (The size of the rectangle should be 48 cm x 10 cm [19 in x 4 in].)

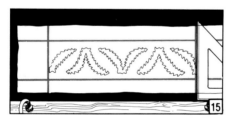

4. Carefully lower the cleaned screen, squeegee-side up, over the cut-outs and butt the long edge against the wood. Using an HB pencil, draw a rectangle on the mesh to match that drawn around the stencil.

5. Turn the screen over and, with the exception of the drawn rectangle, which will be clearly visible through the mesh, cover the whole underside of the screen with packaging tape.

REGISTRATION

Lower the screen over the fabric again, squeegee-side up, and line up the rectangle on the material with the window on the screen. Measure the length of the stencil design (it should be 48 cm [19 in]) and mark off 47.8 cm [$18\frac{11}{12}$ in] lengths on the fabric, starting from the *right-hand* side of the screen and working along the

fabric to the end. (The 2 mm [$\frac{1}{12}$ in] difference is the amount by which the adjoining print should overlap.)

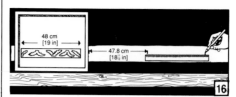

Many of the students I have taught have experienced great difficulty in visualizing the workability of this and the following directions - until they put them into practice. They really work. Just follow the steps and you will see!

PRINTING

1. Spoon ink onto the screen and print the first design (also called a 'repeat').

2. Pick up the screen and put it down one space away from the first so that the lower edge of the frame is against the wood and the *right-hand* edge aligns with the *second* mark on the fabric. (By printing every alternate repeat, there is less chance of putting the screen down on a very wet print.)

3. Return to the beginning and print the even spaces. If the prints either side are still a bit damp, place strips of newspaper over them because if ink is picked up by the underside of the screen it will be transferred as a smudge to the next print. (I often use newspaper in this way, but if the ink is too wet the newspaper will absorb some of it. This can result in a lighter patch of colour on your fabric when it is dry.)

4. Continue printing until all four strips have been completed.

5. Peel off and discard the paper stencil. Pull off all the tape and clean the screen well with water.

The Pink Border

THE FABRIC

1. Cut two strips of fabric measuring 140 cm x 12 cm [55 in x 5 in] and two measuring 190 cm x 12 cm [$74\frac{3}{4}$ in x 5 in]. Spread the first strip on the printing table about 14 cm [$5\frac{1}{2}$ in] away from the wood.

2. Using a fabric marking pen, draw a rectangle 35 cm x 7.5 cm [$13\frac{7}{8}$ in x 3 in] on the extreme left-hand side of a strip, leaving a 2.5 cm [1 in] border top and bottom.

3. Repeat these directions for the remaining three fabric strips.

THE STENCIL

1. Using design (5), trace and cut out four sets of flowers.

2. Cut one flower in half, vertically, as for the green border.

3. Arrange the flowers in the rectangle on one of the fabric strips, opposite ways up, with a half design at either end, ensuring that all the flower pieces are equidistant.

THE SCREEN

1. Lower the cleaned screen over the flowers, butting the long edge against the wood. Using an HB pencil, mark the outline of the rectangle to be printed on the squeegee side of the mesh.

2. Turn the screen upside down and mask off the area surrounding this rectangle with packaging tape.

REGISTRATION

Lower the screen over the fabric again and line up the two rectangles. Measure the length of the repeat, then mark off this measurement along the length of the fabric, starting from the right-hand side of the screen.

PRINTING

Make the first print and continue printing as for the green border until all four strips have been completed.

FINISHING

When the printing has been completed heat-set all the squares and borders.

TO ASSEMBLE THE QUILT

1. Cut a 30 cm [12 in] square window out of a piece of thin card. Place this on the back of each fabric square in turn, centring it over the pattern which should be visible through the fabric.

2. Draw around the inside of the 'window' with a fabric marking pen.

3. Remove the 'window' and add 15 mm [$\frac{5}{8}$ in] all round for the seam allowance, then cut out each square.

4. Join the squares into strips as shown, alternating the colours.

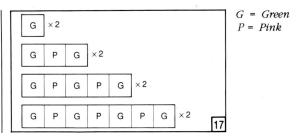

G = Green
P = Pink

5. Now join the strips to form the main body of the quilt.

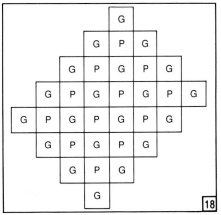

6. Using a fabric marking pen, draw a line through the diagonals of the outside green squares; then draw a second line 15 mm [$\frac{5}{8}$ in] away for the seam allowance. Cut along this line.

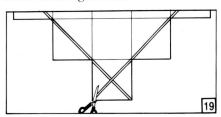

7. Cut strips of plain calico 4.5 cm [$1\frac{3}{4}$ in] wide and sew them all round the quilt, beginning with the short sides first, then the long sides, overlapping them log-cabin style.

8. Similarly, sew on the pink border, then sew on another 4.5 cm-wide [$1\frac{3}{4}$ in-wide] plain border and, finally, sew on the green border and the last plain strips.

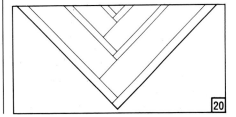

9. Prepare the quilt backing by cutting and joining the fabric so that you have a single piece measuring 240 cm x 190 cm [$94\frac{1}{2}$ in x $74\frac{3}{4}$ in].

10. Lay the backing fabric, right side down, on the floor and smooth a large sheet of batting (wadding) over it. Cover the batting with the quilt front, right side up.

11. Tack the three layers together, beginning in the centre of the quilt and working towards the corners, and then from the centre to the sides. Do at least 32 rows of tacking. (This is very tough on the fingers but worth it in the end.)

12. Machine the quilt along all the seam lines of the joined squares, holding all the layers very firmly behind and in front of the presser foot.

13. Cut off any excess batting (wadding) and backing calico.

14. For the edge trim, cut two strips of calico 220 cm x 12 cm [$86\frac{1}{2}$ in x 5 in] and two strips 170 cm x 12 cm [67 in x 5 in].

15. Fold all four strips in half lengthways and press. (The strips are doubled for strength.)

16. Working on the right side of the quilt, lay the raw edge of the two short calico strips along the two short sides of the quilt and sew them together. Then turn the folded edge of the calico to the back and hem it in position by hand.

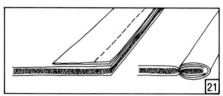

17. Similarly, sew the two remaining calico strips to the two long sides of the quilt, overlapping the trim on the short sides and finishing by hand.

The completed 'Hawaiian Quilt'. If a larger quilt is required, more borders can be added or more squares used.

LANDSCAPE JACKET

The idea for this design came to me while driving past freshly ploughed wheat and barley fields. I was fascinated by all the different stripes of colour: the rich browns of newly turned earth against the black of burnt grass and the faded yellows of remaining stubble, while in the distance soft purple mountains merged into a pale blue sky.

I decided on this design because I wanted a project for all those people who believe they cannot draw. The stripes are created simply by masking off the screen with varying widths of tape. The skill lies in choosing and mixing the colours.

Additional Materials

Masking tape: 24 mm [1 in] and 12 mm [$\frac{1}{2}$ in]
Fabric (for a medium-size, loose-fitting jacket): 2.3 m x 150 cm-wide [$2\frac{1}{2}$ yds x 59 in-wide] calico, or 3.3 m x 120 cm-wide [$3\frac{2}{3}$ yds x 48 in-wide] calico

The Screen

1. Turn the screen so that the underside is facing up. Then, using an HB pencil, draw a 19.2 cm [$7\frac{3}{4}$ in] square in the centre. (Make sure that the corners form right angles.)
2. Carefully stick a length of packaging tape along the outside of the pencil line on each of the four sides.
3. Now cover the mesh between the taped off square and the frame with more tape, overlapping each round by about 5 mm [$\frac{1}{4}$ in] to ensure that no ink seeps through.

Cutting the Fabric

Cut the fabric into the following pieces:
For the back, one piece 102 cm x 82 cm [$40\frac{1}{4}$ in x $32\frac{1}{2}$ in].
For the front, two pieces 102 cm x 50 cm [$40\frac{1}{4}$ in x 20 in].
For the sleeves, two pieces 64 cm x 64 cm [$25\frac{1}{4}$ in x $25\frac{1}{4}$ in]
For the collar, one piece 64 cm x 24 cm [$25\frac{1}{4}$ in x $9\frac{1}{2}$ in].

The Colours

1. For the *grey*, mix 250 ml [9 fl oz] clear base with 3 ml [$\frac{1}{2}$ tsp] magenta, 3 ml [$\frac{1}{2}$ tsp] azure, 5 ml [1 tsp] primrose and 3 ml [$\frac{1}{2}$ tsp] black.
2. For the *blue*, mix 250 ml [9 fl oz] clear base with 10 ml [2 tsp] azure, 4 m [$\frac{3}{4}$ tsp] magenta and 1 ml [$\frac{1}{4}$ tsp] primrose.
3. For the *beige*, mix 250 ml [9 fl oz] clear base with 10 ml [2 tsp] primrose, 10 ml [2 tsp] azure, 10 ml [2 tsp] magenta.
4. For the *orange*, mix 250 ml [9 fl oz] clear base with 60 ml [4 tbsp] primrose, 7 ml [$1\frac{1}{2}$ tsp] azure and 10 ml [2 tsp] magenta.
5. For the *brown*, mix 250 ml [9 fl oz] clear base with 60 ml [4 tbsp] primrose and 30 ml [2 tbsp] each of azure and magenta.
6. For the *ochre*, mix 250 ml [9 fl oz] clear base, 15 ml [1 tbsp] primrose, 15 ml [1 tbsp] azure, 5 ml [1 tsp] magenta and 3 ml [$\frac{1}{2}$ tsp] black
7. *Black* is used as supplied.

Label each jar of prepared colour and number them 1 to 7.

THE BACK

The Fabric

1. Fold the fabric for the back in half lengthways and match up the corners. Score the fold with your fingernail.
2. Press the lower half of the folded fabric onto the printing table, then smooth the fabric from the centre to the edges to eliminate wrinkles or air bubbles.
3. Open out the fabric carefully and smooth the other side flat.

Registration

1. Mark the centre fold with a fabric marking pen or a chalk-line and mark two lines on either side 19 cm [7½ in] away from the centre fold.

2. Using a fabric marking pen and starting 2.5 cm [1 in] from the bottom, mark six lengths of 19 cm [7½ in] up both selvedges and join them across the fabric with a chalk line. There will be 20 squares, each measuring 19 cm [7½ in]. These squares will be smaller than the square on your screen so that the prints overlap slightly to prevent the background colour showing in between.

3. With a fabric marking pen, and following diagram 22, write in each square the number of the colour to be printed there. (These numbers will disappear when you print onto them.)

Printing
ALL-OVER COLOUR

1. Place the screen over the square to be printed grey in the lowest row. Look through the mesh and you will see the lines you drew. Position the screen so that the lines on the fabric lie just inside the tape on the screen.

2. Ladle about 60 ml [4 tbsp] *pale grey* ink onto the screen on the far side of the square, making sure that none of it falls on the printing square.

3. Hold the squeegee at a 45° angle and pull the ink gently over the square towards you. Pull the squeegee towards you again, this time very firmly.

4. Print the other two pale grey squares.

5. Using a small piece of cardboard, scrape as much ink off the screen as possible and return it to the jar. Do the same with the squeegee. If the colours are quite similar it is not necessary to wash the screen. (I printed all six colours before washing the screen.)

6. Continue printing the squares in their numbered sequence. If the screen overlaps a recently printed square, dry the print with a hair dryer for a minute or so until the shine has gone.

7. Without removing the packaging tape that surrounds the square, clean the screen thoroughly, using a scrubbing brush and a little non-abrasive household cleaner to shift any stubborn ink. Rinse well and leave to dry.

Now it is time to overprint the squares with different colour stripes.

THE FOUR-STRIPE SQUARES

1. Divide the printing aperture on the screen into four by sticking two 48 mm-wide [2 in-wide] pieces of packaging tape to the screen to form stripes. (One piece touches one side of the square and two stripes are left open to print.)

2. With diagram 23 as a guide, print the *blue* square first. (Looking through the mesh, it is easy to position the screen exactly over the original grey square.)

3. Next, print the *beige* stripes but dry the first square with a hair dryer before printing the second one as they are so close together. Dry the second set of beige stripes.

4. Next, print the *brown* stripes.

5. Remove the packaging tape used for the stripes and clean the screen thoroughly. (Do not remove the packaging tape that forms the square.)

THE EIGHT-STRIPE SQUARES

1. Using 24 mm [1 in] masking tape, mask off the four stripes. You will now have four open areas of mesh measuring the full width of the square by 24 mm [1 in].

2. Following diagram 24, print the *black* stripes, then the *blue, brown* and *ochre* stripes. It may seem strange to be printing black on black, but it makes an intense black which adds interest to a rather flat area.

3. Remove the masking tape and wash the screen thoroughly.

THE SIXTEEN-STRIPE SQUARES

1. Stick eight pieces of narrow (12 mm [½ in]) masking tape onto the screen so that you have 16 stripes in all.

2. Following diagram 25, overprint the remaining squares.

FRONT, SLEEVES AND COLLAR

THE FRONT

The arrangement of the squares is exactly the same as for the back but each front is printed on a separate piece of fabric, leaving a 10 cm-wide [4 in-wide] border on either side of the centre.

In addition, print two borders in a continuous *blue* and overprint with the 16-stripe square in the same blue.

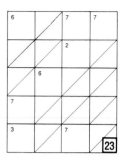

Colour Key
1. = grey
2. = blue
3. = beige
4. = orange
5. = brown
6. = ochre
7. = black

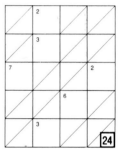

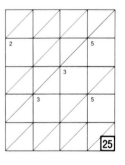

THE SLEEVES

Only nine squares are needed for the sleeves and these are arranged in a square (three by three). Print them in the same colours that were used for the lower right-hand corner of the back.

THE COLLAR

Print three squares in *blue*, then overprint each square with the 16-stripe square in the same blue.

Finishing

When all the printing has been completed, heat-set the fabric.

TO ASSEMBLE THE JACKET

Find a pattern with a loose, unstructured shape (Butterick pattern 6082 is ideal) and make up the jacket accordingly. The pockets and lapels of the jacket pictured below were made with a co-ordinating plain fabric, with rust tape appliquéd over them. The buttons were hand-made from terracotta-coloured clay.

For the lining I chose the 'Guineafowl' design (see page 70), but if you have not progressed to light-sensitive screens yet, either buy a colour co-ordinated fabric or sponge-paint a matching one.

'Landscape Jacket', front and back. Here imaginative use of colour demonstrates how a very simple design can result in a most unusual jacket for casual wear.

FRIENDSHIP QUILT

A teacher from my children's school asked if I would like to give a series of screen printing lessons to my daughter's class. I jumped at the opportunity.

The aim of the project was to print curtains for the seniors' dining room. For their stencils the children chose a variety of subjects drawn from the school environment: the owls that return to nest in the old oak tree every year, the gable of the old homestead, the school bell and many other aspects of the school that were special to them. Their designs were so fresh and innovative that, when they were printing the curtains, I asked them to print one of each design on a separate piece of cotton so that I could make them into a quilt for my daughter, Linda. Every square on the quilt is different and today is a constant reminder to Linda of her friends from primary school.

This is not necessarily a children's project. I think a 'friendship quilt' would be a warm and wonderful present for a group of friends to give to someone on a special occasion. Every person in the group could make a small scene to remind their friend of an event that they had shared. One or two people could join the squares, then everyone could get together to quilt them.

Additional Materials

Fabric (to make a 225 cm x 180 cm [87½ in in x 71 in] single or three-quarter bed quilt):

For the squares — 2.5 m x 150 cm-wide [2¾ yds x 59 in-wide], or 3 m x 120 cm-wide [3¼ yds x 48 in-wide] white medium-weight cotton

For the backing and sashing — 5 m x 150 cm-wide [5½ yds x 59 in-wide], or 7 m x 120 cm-wide [7½ yds x 48 in-wide] colour co-ordinating medium-weight cotton

Batting (wadding) — 235 cm x 190 cm [92½ in x 75 in]

For the border: 2 m x 150 cm-wide or 120 cm-wide [2¼ yds x 59 in-wide or 48 in-wide] navy blue medium-weight cotton

For the trimming — 8 m x 6 cm-wide [8¾ yds x 2½ in-wide] white cotton lace

THE SQUARES

The Stencils

Draw your design on a piece of paper 18 cm [7 in] square. With scissors or a craft knife cut out all those areas you want the ink to go through and print.

The Screen

On the underside of the screen draw an 18 cm [7 in] square with an HB pencil. Surround this area with packaging tape, overlapping the layers slightly so that the ink does not squeeze through.

The Colour

For the *blue*, mix 250 ml [9 fl oz] clear base with 250 ml [9 fl oz] azure, 60 ml [4 tbsp] magenta and 30 ml [2 tbsp] primrose. Stir well and test before using.

The Fabric

Cut or tear the fabric into 25 cm [10 in] squares. You will need 48 altogether. (If that number seems a bit daunting, you could re-design the quilt using much larger squares.)

Registration

1. With a fabric marking pen, draw an 18 cm [7 in] square on one of the square pieces of fabric.

2. Place the fabric square on the printing table and mark all four corners on the table with masking tape so that each subsequent square can be positioned in precisely the same place.

3. Lower the screen over the fabric square, carefully lining it up with the drawn square. Now, stick more masking tape on the printing table to mark the four corners of the screen so that it, too, can be positioned in precisely the same place every time you print. Remove the screen.

Printing

1. Place one of the paper stencils on the marked fabric square on the table, carefully arranging all the loose bits of paper where you want them. (One child at school had cut out a tree trunk and 43 tiny oak leaves! It took a long time to lay them all out but it made a beautiful print.)
2. With the masking tape as a guide, gently lower the screen over the stencil, taking care not to disturb the paper.
3. Spoon on the blue ink and print with the squeegee.
4. Remove the screen, lifting up one side first. The paper will have stuck to it and you will have printed the first square.
5. When you have printed 48 squares, leave them to dry, then heat-set them. (Such small squares can easily be heat-set with a hot iron.)

TO ASSEMBLE THE QUILT

For the backing and sashing I bought a blue and white co-ordinating fabric with a delightful butterfly design.

1. Cut and sew the backing fabric to make a rectangle measuring 235 cm x 190 cm [92 in x 75 in]
2. For the sashing, cut from the remaining co-ordinating fabric:
Forty 20 cm x 7 cm-wide [8 in x $2\frac{3}{4}$ in-wide] strips.
Nine 135 cm x 7 cm-wide [$53\frac{1}{4}$ x $2\frac{3}{4}$ in-wide] strips.
Two 189 cm x 7 cm-wide [$74\frac{1}{2}$ x $2\frac{3}{4}$ in-wide] strips.
3. Trim all of the squares, leaving a 1 cm [$\frac{3}{8}$ in] seam allowance all round each 18 cm [7 in] printed square.
4. Place all of the squares on the floor (six across by eight down) and decide how you want to arrange them.
5. Join together the squares in every horizontal row with a short (20 cm [8 in]) strip of sashing in between each one.
6. Next, take a piece of sashing measuring 135 cm [$53\frac{1}{4}$ in] in length and place it along the top edge of the bottom row of

joined squares (right sides together). Tack the two together, leaving a 1 cm [$\frac{3}{8}$ in] seam allowance, and then sew them.
7. Repeat this procedure with the next rows of joined squares. Then sew all the rows together.
8. Now attach a piece of sashing around all four sides of the joined squares, the two remaining shorter lengths along the top and bottom edges and the two longer lengths along the sides, overlapping them log-cabin style.
9. Press all the seams flat.
10. From the navy blue fabric, cut:
Two strips measuring 145 cm x 20 cm [$57\frac{1}{4}$ in x 8 in].
Two strips measuring 225 cm x 20 cm [$88\frac{1}{2}$ in x 8 in].
Sew these strips around the pieced section, starting with the two short sides and so that the two long sides overlap them.
11. Sew the lace along the middle of the strip of navy fabric all round the quilt. Sew it by machine along the straight edge and by hand along the fuller edge, gathering and easing it around the corners so that it lies flat.
12. Tack and machine-quilt together the backing, batting (wadding) and pieced top as for 'Ndebele Quilt' (see page 58).
13. Cut off any excess batting (wadding) and backing.
14. From the remaining backing and sashing fabric, cut as many 6 cm-wide [$2\frac{1}{2}$ in-wide] strips to edge the quilt, as were used in 'Hawaiian Quilt' (see page 29).

> **NOTE**
> The quilt that is illustrated was edged slightly differently, using strips cut on the bias, but this requires a great deal more fabric.

The idea of 'friendship squares' need not be limited to a quilt: a 'friendship cushion' makes an equally special gift.

LEAVES

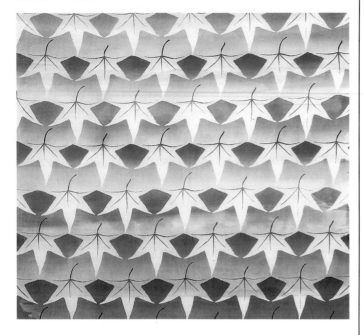

This design was inspired by plane tree leaves picked by my son, Matthew. The intricate, yet simple, shape of these leaves was perfect for a paper stencil.

I wanted a very soft look, so I worked out a method of printing the colours so that they graduated from white to dark blue across a single leaf. Any other colours, however, such as maroon, through red to rust, could be used as successfully.

Additional Materials
Sellotape
Suggested fabric: fine muslin
Design: (6) on page 84

The Stencil
1. Using a photocopier, enlarge the leaf design to measure 41 cm x 23 cm [16 in x 9 in] and cut it out.
2. Trace the design onto brown paper, then cut it out with a pair of scissors. Remove the leaf veins with a craft knife.

The Screen
1. On the underside of the screen, stick one width of packaging tape all around the outside edge, slightly overlapping the frame, so that the area of mesh is reduced to 41 cm x 36 cm [16 in x 14 in].
2. Using Sellotape, tape the paper stencil of the leaves along the length of the

> **—— NOTE ——**
> You could as easily print this design using a leaf from your own garden.

underside of the screen with the straight edge of the stencil slightly overlapping the packaging tape.

The Colours
1. For the *dark blue*, mix 125 ml [$4\frac{1}{2}$ fl oz] clear base with 125 ml [$4\frac{1}{2}$ fl oz] azure, 30 ml [2 tbsp] magenta and 10 ml [2 tsp] primrose.
2. For the *medium blue*, mix 125 ml [$4\frac{1}{2}$ fl oz] dark blue with 125 ml [$4\frac{1}{2}$ fl oz] clear base.
3. For the *light blue*, mix 125 ml [$4\frac{1}{2}$ fl oz] medium blue with 125 ml [$4\frac{1}{2}$ fl oz] clear base.

Registration
1. Spread out the fabric on your printing table and, if you are using the design from this book, mark off 15 cm [6 in] distances (the height of each leaf, excluding the stalk) along both selvedges.
2. Using a chalk line, join the marks across the width of the fabric.
3. Place the screen on the fabric so that the chalk line runs through the bottom of the leaves and mark both sides of the frame where the line intersects it.

Printing
This all-over design is printed as a border (see page 18).

1. Start printing on the left-hand side of the first (bottom) line. Spoon about 15 ml [1 tbsp] of *dark blue* ink close to the base of the leaf on the right-hand side of the screen, then spoon 15 ml [1 tbsp] of *medium blue* immediately above the dark blue, and then 15 ml [1 tbsp] of *light blue*. (This should come to the height of the point of the leaf.) Place a blob of *clear base* just beyond the point of the leaf to prevent a definite line of colour on the edge of the print.

2. Pull the squeegee over the screen firmly two or three times. On the first print the lines will be fairly definite, but on subsequent prints the colours will merge to create a subtle gradation.

3. Lift the screen carefully and make the next print, slightly overlapping the first, but make sure that the adjoining printed edge is dry or covered with newspaper, otherwise there may be some smudging. Complete the first row.

4. Miss the next horizontal chalk line and print every *alternate* row until you reach the end of the fabric.

5. Peel off the stencil and discard it. Clean the screen thoroughly.

6. Cut a new leaf stencil while the fabric is drying, then place it on the fabric so that the tip of each leaf points at the space between the leaves on the row above.

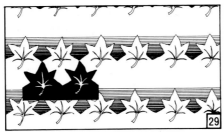

7. Place the screen over the stencil so that the straight edge of the stencil just overlaps the tape on the long side of the screen. Mark the screen where the chalk line intersects it.

8. Spoon on the ink as you did previously and print the intermediate rows. (After the first print, turn the screen over and tape the stencil onto the screen along the straight edge of the leaf stencil. This stops the ink seeping through.)

9. When all the printing has been completed, clean the screen thoroughly.

Finishing
When the ink is dry, heat-set the fabric.

The subtle gradation of colour achieved in printing these leaves is a further example of how a very simple technique can transform an unremarkable pattern into a sophisticated designer fabric.

CHAPTER THREE

PAINTED SCREENS

One of the wonderful things about screen printing is that there is a technique to suit everybody. The painted screen will appeal particularly to those who like painting. In this technique bituminous-based paint or a proprietary filler is applied to various parts of the screen to block up the mesh and stop the ink from passing through when the squeegee is pulled over the surface. These fillers can either be painted directly onto the mesh, as in 'Little Flowers' and 'Key Design' (see pages 40 and 42), or over a 'resist', as in 'The Enchanted Forest' and 'Ashanti Prints' (see pages 43 and 46).

Painted screens also introduce the need for a different method of cleaning the mesh. Working out-of-doors, lay the coated screen underside down on newspaper. If the screen has been coated with *bituminous paint*, pour *mineral turpentine* over the mesh. Leave it to soak for about 10 minutes, keeping the mesh constantly damp with the turpentine. Similarly, if the screen has been coated with a *proprietary filler*, pour a generous quantity of *thinners* over the mesh and leave it to soak.

After 10 minutes the mesh fillers will have softened considerably. Wipe off as much as possible using paper towel (kitchen paper). To remove persistent filler, place the screen on more newspaper and pour on a little *Autosolve*. Work it into the mesh with a dish washing brush and leave it for 2 to 3 minutes; then rub a little *Autopaste* onto both sides of the mesh. Again, leave it for 2 to 3 minutes. Finally, hose off the chemicals with a very hard jet of water and leave the screen to dry.

Basic materials: screen (61 cm x 56 cm [24 in x 22 in]); squeegee (46 cm [18 in]) long; textile printing inks (magenta, azure, primrose, black and clear base); HB pencil; ruler; thinners or mineral turpentine; packaging tape, Autopaste and Autosolve.

(Opposite) The fabric designs featured on this skirt are the African 'Ashanti Prints' and the 'Ndebele Quilt' border. (Above) Ideas for fabric designs are all around us. The 'Key Design' on this children's T-shirt originated in the border of a Belouchi rug.

LITTLE FLOWERS

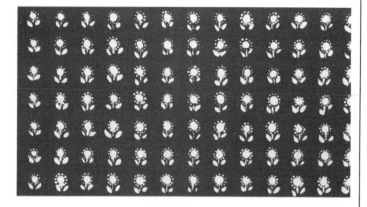

I designed this pattern because I wanted a small print with a dark background to co-ordinate with 'Hawaiian Quilt' (see page 26) and the 'Persian Flowers' design that I printed on calico (see page 75). It highlights, however, one of the shortcomings of screen printing: that is, in a repeat where the background is being printed, you can see a darker line where the two prints overlap.

There are three ways to overcome this problem. The design can be printed:
1. on separate pieces of fabric which are later joined together, then quilted onto batting (wadding) so that the seam is not noticeable (see the cushion cover illustrated above);
2. on a continuous piece of fabric but as separate blocks with a border of un-printed fabric all round; or
3. in black, so that the overlap is not noticeable.

Additional Materials

Water colour brush: size 3
Bituminous paint (available from a
 hardware shop)
Fabric (to make a 53 cm-square [21
 in-square] cushion cover):
 For printing – 4 pieces of calico, each
 34 cm [$13\frac{1}{2}$ in] square
 Batting (wadding) – 59 cm [24 in]
 square
 For the backing and bias strip – 1 m x
 150 cm-wide [1 yd x 59 in-wide] or
 $1\frac{1}{4}$ m x 120 cm-wide [$1\frac{1}{4}$ yds x 48-in
 wide] calico
 For the piping – 2.25 m x 5 mm-thick
 [$2\frac{1}{2}$ yds x $\frac{1}{4}$ in-thick] cotton string or
 cord

The Screen

1. Using an HB pencil, draw a 28 cm [11 in] square on the underside of the screen and surround it with packaging tape. Then tape the rest of the open mesh between the square and the frame, overlapping each layer.

2. In pencil, draw a 1 cm-wide [$\frac{3}{8}$ in-wide] border around the inside of the taped off square; then divide the rest of the open mesh into a grid of 2 cm [$\frac{3}{4}$ in] squares (13 across x 13 down).

3. At the intersection of each line paint a large dot of bituminous paint. (This will be the centre of the flower.) Around it paint as many little dots as will fit, but do not make them too small or they will disappear when you print them.

4. Paint the stalks with a fine brush stroke and the leaves with two fat strokes. (It is not necessary to make all the flowers identical. The design is far more interesting if they are all slightly different.)

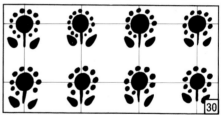

5. As bituminous paint takes a long time to dry, leave it overnight. (Even after 12 hours it will feel quite tacky, but it will not smudge on the fabric.)

The Colour

For the *pink*, mix 250 ml [9 fl oz] clear base with 15 ml [1 tbsp] magenta, 2.5 ml [$\frac{1}{2}$ tsp] azure and 1 ml [$\frac{1}{4}$ tsp] primrose.

The Fabric

I printed this design on separate squares but below are three possible methods for preparing and registering the fabric.
For separate squares: Tear or cut the fabric into 34 cm [$13\frac{1}{2}$ in] squares, then place the squares on the printing table far enough apart to avoid the screen

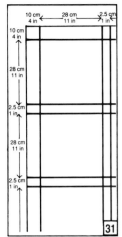

being placed on an adjacent wet print.

For squares with a plain fabric border: Mark out the fabric according to diagram 31, remembering that the size of the squares is 28 cm [11 in] and the space between them is 2.5 cm [1 in].

For a continuous print: Mark out the fabric as instructed in 'Registration: an all-over design' on page 18. The distance between the lines in both directions will be 27.8 cm [$10\frac{11}{12}$ in], allowing for a 2 mm [$\frac{1}{12}$ in] overlap.

Printing

1. Place the screen, squeegee-side up, over a fabric square and spoon on the ink. (Because the dots I painted on my screen were on the small side, I could only pull the squeegee over once, otherwise some of the dots would have disappeared. It is therefore important to make sure that there is enough ink at the top of the screen before you start so that one firm pull of the squeegee is all you will need to cover the screen completely.)

2. Print the other three squares.

3. Heat-set the squares with a hot iron.

To Make the Cushion Cover

THE PRINTED SIDE

1. Join the squares together so that none of the white fabric shows between the four squares. Trim the outside seam allowance to 1.5 cm [$\frac{5}{8}$ in] all round.

2. Cut a piece of plain muslin or calico the same size as the four joined squares, plus an additional 3 cm [1.5 in] for a seam allowance (ie 59 cm [$23\frac{1}{4}$ in] square).

3. On top of this place a piece of batting

'Little Flowers' is an ideal mix-and-match design and could be printed in any colour. Here it complements 'Persian Flowers', right, and the 'Hawaiian Quilt'.

(wadding) the same size and cover it with the joined printed squares.

4. Tack these together well, then machine-quilt between every second row of flowers in both directions.

TO PREPARE THE CUSHION BACKING

This cushion is made with a deep overlap at the back, so no fastenings are needed.

1. Cut two pieces of backing material 59 cm x 42 cm [$23\frac{1}{2}$ in x $16\frac{1}{4}$ in].

2. Sew a 2.5 cm [1 in] hem along one of the long sides of each piece of backing fabric.

THE PIPING

Although bias strips use a lot of material, piping really gives a professional finish to a cushion.

1. Cut 2.25 m [$2\frac{1}{2}$ yds] of bias strip 4 cm [$1\frac{5}{8}$ in] wide and the same length of thick cotton string or cord.

2. Place the cord down the centre of the bias strip. Fold the strip over and tack it close to the cord.

ASSEMBLING THE PIECES

1. Tack the piping to the right side of the printed top, raw edges outwards, letting the two ends of the piping meet on a straight edge rather than on a corner.

2. Clip the bias strip at the four corners so that it lies flat.

3. Where the two ends of the piping meet, cut one off at right angles to the edge and cut the cord only of the other side so that it butts exactly against the other piece of cord. Then cut the remaining bias 1.5 cm [$\frac{5}{8}$ in] longer.

4. Turn in and hem the overlapping piece of bias, then wrap it around the other end. Tack it in place. (This makes an almost invisible join in the piping.)

5. Place the two pieces of backing fabric, right side down, face to face with the printed square. (The two backing pieces should overlap in the centre.)

6. Tack the printed square and the backing together along the edge of the piping. Then, using the zipper foot of your machine, sew as close as possible to the outside edge of the piping.

7. Turn the cushion cover right side out and it is ready to use.

KEY DESIGN

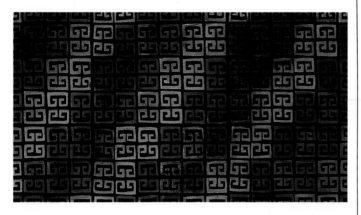

For this project I needed to cover two loose cushions on an old Morris chair, so I bought a coarser, stronger cotton than I normally use. If you, too, wish to use this design for covering cushions, you will have to take your own measurements.

Additional Materials

Bituminous paint
Water colour brush: size 3
Paint brush: 2.5 cm [1 in] wide (bristle length halved)
Pieces of foam sponge
Fabric: own choice
Design: (7) on page 85

The Screen

1. With an HB pencil, draw a rectangle 29 cm across x 28 cm down [$11\frac{1}{2}$ in across x 11 in down] on the underside of the screen, then surround it with strips of packaging tape to block off the rest of the mesh.
2. Divide the printing area into 24 blocks (four across by six down), each measuring 7 cm x 4.8 cm [$2\frac{3}{4}$ in x 2 in].
3. Enlarge the design on a photocopier.
4. Lay the screen, squeegee-side up, over the design so that a single motif fits into each of the small rectangles, then trace them onto the mesh with a pencil.
5. Working on the underside of the screen, paint bituminous paint onto the areas that are black in the design. (This is a slow process, so relax, enjoy it and do not feel that all the rectangles have to be identical.).
6. When you have finished painting the design, hold the screen up to the light to check for pinholes in the paint and fill them in wherever you see them. Leave the screen to dry.

The Colours

I printed this design in *black*, and, as background colour, used *five shades of brown* taken from the warm side of the colour wheel.

For these you will need purple (no. 8), magenta (no. 9), scarlet (no. 10), orange (no. 11) and yellow orange (no. 12). To each one is added a small quantity of its complementary colour. To lighten the inks, add four parts of clear base to every one part of colour.

As these inks are to be brushed on after printing, dilute them by adding 25% water. Stir well.

Registration

Follow the instructions for registering an all-over design given on page 18, marking out the repeats every 28.8 cm [$11\frac{3}{8}$ in] along the selvedges and every 27.8 cm [$10\frac{7}{8}$ in] along the cut edges.

Printing

Print the fabric following the instructions given for printing on page 20.

I used my 32 mesh screen for the first time in this project. It was very easy to print through. There was no clogging, which you get with a very fine mesh, and the layer of ink deposited was very even. The one disadvantage is that the curves become 'stepped', making a slightly cruder print. This will be suitable for some designs but not for others. (There is no special need to use a coarse mesh for this design. Your normal 43 mesh will print this design just as well, if not better.)

Finishing

1. Partially heat-set the printed fabric (see page 21).
2. Take the five prepared shades of brown ink and, using a thick paint brush, dab them generously onto the design in diagonal lines.
3. After each set of five lines, wipe off the excess paint with a clean sponge. (The lines of colour tend to overlap when you apply the inks and blend as you wipe them with the sponge. This adds to the richness of the design.)
4. Heat-set the fabric before making up.

THE ENCHANTED FOREST

I was so thrilled by the children's response to paper stencils in the 'Friendship Squares' project (see 'Friendship Quilt' on page 34) that I was interested to see whether we could take screen printing a step further. The two designs in this project were done entirely by my daughter, Linda, and her friend, Katharine, when they were 12 years old. I think they are wonderful - and the potential for this type of screen preparation is endless.

The 'resist' method used is easy and direct. First, the design to be printed is painted onto the mesh with a water-soluble paint (the 'resist'), then the entire mesh is coated with a thinners-based proprietary filler (available at all screen printing suppliers). After this the paint is sprayed with water until it dissolves and is washed away, leaving the mesh open only in those areas where the paint once was. This way, it is the design that was painted onto the screen that eventually prints, unlike the previous two projects where the painted areas did not allow the ink to pass through.

Additional Materials

Paper: 40 cm (15¾ in) squares (as many as are required)
Charcoal
White powder paint
Paint brush: 1.25 cm [½ in] hog's hair brush
Filler: a thinners-based proprietary filler
Stiff cardboard: about 5 cm x 10 cm [2 in x 4 in]
Fabric marking pen
Chalk line
Fabric: own choice

— NOTE —
Never substitute acrylic poster paints for powder paint when using the 'resist' technique.

The Design

Take a square piece of paper and make a rough sketch. (For this project I asked the children to draw an enchanted forest full of strange animals and creepy crawlies. We used charcoal so that their drawings did not become small and fiddly as they tend to with pencil.)

The Screen

My purpose in preparing a screen in the following way was to use materials familiar to the children from their school art classes.

1. Place the screen, underside up, on the table. Place the drawing on the mesh as centrally as possible and carefully draw around it with a ruler and a blunt HB pencil so that you have a 40 cm [15¾ in] square on the mesh.

2. Fill in the area between the drawn square and the frame of the screen with overlapping strips of packaging tape.

3. Now turn the screen squeegee-side up, slip the drawing underneath and again, using charcoal (never use oil pastels as they clog the mesh), 'trace' your drawing onto the printing area of the screen.

4. Mix the white powder paint with sufficient water to produce a consistency similar to that of stirred yoghurt. (If it is too thick it is difficult to handle. If it is too thin it does not resist the filler and all your work will be in vain.)

5. Turn the screen underside up again and, using the prepared powder paint, paint over all the areas you want to print. (The charcoal outline of the drawing will be clearly visible through the mesh.) Make sure that the shapes of the unpainted areas are as interesting as your pattern. Do not worry if the outlines are not perfectly smooth - it is the brush marks that give this type of screen print its special quality.

6. Let the paint dry completely before moving on to the next step. (This should take 30 minutes on a dry day.)

7. The entire surface of the underside of the mesh, including the painted areas, must now be covered with filler. To do this, pour a puddle of filler about 3 cm [1¼ in] in diameter onto the packaging tape. Take the 5 cm x 10 cm-wide [2 in x 4 in-wide] piece of cardboard and, holding it at right angles to the screen, pull the filler firmly across the surface of the mesh towards you. Repeat this process until the entire surface is covered.

NOTE
Be careful not to slope the cardboard towards you as if you were using the squeegee, because a 45° angle will cause the filler to be pushed through the mesh instead of drawing it over the surface.

---

8. Hold the screen up to the light to check that there are no gaps in the filler. If you can see pinholes of light in the filled areas, apply filler with a paint brush. Leave it to dry thoroughly (about 10 minutes).

9. Take the screen to the bathroom, or outside to the garden hose, and gently spray the squeegee side of the screen with water. You will see the powder paint begin to dissolve and run down the screen. (This is why acrylic poster colour cannot be used - it does not dissolve in water.)

10. When most of the paint has dissolved, you will notice that the paint has stopped the filler reaching the mesh and the filler that was pulled over the painted areas has been sprayed off. To dislodge the last unwanted bits of filler, scrub the back of the mesh (the underside) with a scrubbing brush or nail brush. Do not be afraid to scrub hard.

11. Leave the screen to dry.

The Colours

I printed these designs in a dark blue and then sponged over them with greens, turquoises and purple.

For the *dark blue*, mix 250 ml [9 fl oz] azure with 250 ml [9 fl oz] clear base, then add 30 ml [2 tbsp] magenta and 15 ml [1 tbsp] primrose.

Using the instructions for colour mixing given in chapter one (see page 14), have fun mixing your own colours for sponging on. Just remember to add at least three times more clear base than colour, otherwise the strength of the inks will obscure the design. Also remember to dilute your final colour mixes with 25% water so that they spread evenly.

Registration

1. Smooth out your fabric on the printing table, then, with a fabric marking pen, mark 40 cm [$15\frac{3}{4}$ in] distances along the width and length of the fabric.

2. Using a chalk line, join up the opposite marks on the fabric to make a grid of 40 cm [$15\frac{3}{4}$ in] squares.

3. Place your screen on the fabric and line up the square of the printing aperture with a square on the fabric. Mark your frame where the chalk lines intersect it. (See 'Registration: an all-over design' on page 18).

Printing

Squares can be printed onto a continuous piece of fabric in a variety of configurations. All of the following possibilities should be considered:

1. The most obvious would be to print the design the same way up in rows running across the fabric.

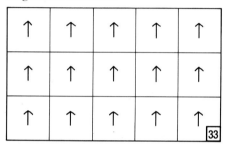

2. Or the even rows could be staggered:

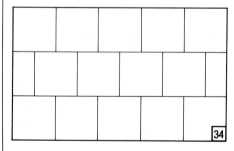

i) Mark out the fabric with the same 40 cm (15¾ in) grid.

ii) Print every other row as if you were following diagram 33.

iii) Print the remaining rows by placing the screen so that the vertical chalk line runs through the centre of your printing aperture. This way the frame will only have contact with one chalk line top and bottom. (Be sure to mark the two points of intersection on the frame, top and bottom, as a guide to screen placement before printing these staggered rows.)

3. The pattern could be printed in blocks of four, with each block facing in a different direction:

i) Starting at the top left-hand corner of the fabric, make one print.

ii) Give the screen a quarter turn in a clockwise direction and make another print next to the first.

iii) Give the screen another quarter turn and print the square immediately below the second.

iv) Give the screen a final quarter turn and print the square immediately below the first.

4. Another option is to change the direction of the pattern, square by square, as you print across one row. (In other words, printing from the left, one row at a time, give the screen a quarter turn in a clockwise direction each time you move to the next square.)

5. For a more all-over look where the repeat is not too obvious, try the method illustrated below:

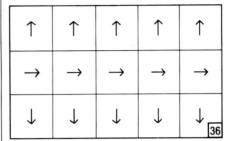

It is clear from these examples that a whole variety of compositions is possible using a single design.

Finishing

These prints look most effective on white. Alternatively, other colours can be sponged on (see page 53) evenly, randomly, in stripes or squares. If you are going to sponge on additional colour, be sure that the printed fabric is thoroughly dry first (see page 21). Then, when all the sponging has been completed, heat-set the fabric.

Linda's design which uses yet another printing sequence.

Katharine's design, which uses the fourth printing sequence outlined above.

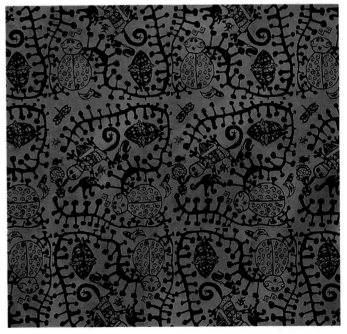

ASHANTI PRINTS

I am fascinated by the symbols used on the Adinkra cloths worn by the Ashanti in Ghana: each one has a name and a mystical meaning.

Because the individual designs are quite small, I wanted many identical shapes on my screen. I could have drawn one and photocopied it many times to repeat it for a light-sensitive positive, but it would have lost its character, so I decided I would have to devise a way of 'block printing' the symbols onto the screen. This I did by making up little felt printing blocks for each one that I wanted to use.

Additional Materials

2 screens (3 in total): each measuring 61 cm x 56 cm [24 in x 22 in]
Tracing paper
Scissors
Craft knife
Cutting board
Light-coloured felt: 30 cm [12 in] square
Sheet of stiff card
Glue
Stiff cardboard: about 5 cm x 10 cm [2 in x 4 in] wide
Contact adhesive
White powder paint
Paint brush: 2.5 cm [1 in] wide (bristle length halved)
Filler: a proprietary thinners-based filler or bituminous paint
Suggested fabric: 120 cm-wide [48 in-wide] cotton
Designs: (8), (9) and (10) on page 86

The Design

1. Trace all three designs, then cut out a paper pattern for each, using a craft knife to cut out the open areas.
2. Place the first pattern on the felt and draw round the shape with a pencil. Repeat this twice more so that you have three separate but identical shapes outlined on the felt.
3. Cut them out. You will be able to use scissors on the outside edges, but again, you will need to cut out the open areas with a craft knife.
4. Glue the three pieces one on top of the other and then stick a piece of card, cut to the same shape, on top of the block to stiffen it.
5. Prepare blocks for the other two designs in the same way.
6. A printing block is much easier to manage if it has a handle, so for each one cut a piece of stiff card into a strip about 5 cm x 2 cm [2 in x $\frac{3}{4}$ in], fold it in half, then fold the ends back to the top. Glue the flaps to the top of a block and it is ready to use.

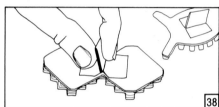

The Screens

SCREEN 1
1. Take the first printing block:
This design is to be repeated eight times across the width of the screen and four times down the length – a total area of 38 cm x 40 cm [15 in x 15$\frac{3}{4}$ in], allowing for a small space between each motif.

Using an HB pencil, draw a rectangle the same size in the centre of the underside of the screen.
2. Mix the powder paint with water until it is the consistency of stirred yoghurt (see Step 4 on page 43).
3. Using a paint brush, apply a thick layer to the printing block and test-print it on the underside of the mesh on the very edge of the screen. If the print has an even layer of paint and an even edge, start printing inside the rectangle you have just drawn.

DESIGN (8)

This motif is printed on clothes to give the wearer security in the home.

DESIGN (9)

This motif represents the Ashanti chair, the sun and the moon, which in turn represent the whole universe.

DESIGN (10)

This motif signifies that the wearer has knowledge.

4. 'Print' all 32 repeat designs, then leave the paint to dry (15 to 30 minutes).

SCREEN 2

1. Take the second printing block:
This time the design is to be repeated six times across the width of the screen and 10 times down the length - an area of 39 cm x 40 cm [$15\frac{3}{8}$ in x $15\frac{3}{4}$ in], allowing for a small space between each individual design.

Draw a rectangle the same size in the centre of the underside of the mesh.
2. Fill the rectangle with the designs as directed for Screen 1 and leave it to dry.

SCREEN 3

1. Take the third printing block:
This motif is to be repeated seven times across the width of the screen and eight times down – an area of 35 cm x 42.5 cm [$13\frac{3}{4}$ in x $16\frac{3}{4}$ in].

Draw a rectangle the same size in the centre of the underside of the mesh.
2. Fill the rectangle with block-printed designs as directed for Screen 1 and leave it to dry.

When the paint is thoroughly dry on all three screens:
1. Spread filler over the entire surface of the underside of each screen.
2. Once the filler is dry, wash off the paint and the unwanted filler following the instructions given in 'The Enchanted Forest' project (see Step 9 of 'The Screen' on page 44).

The Colours

The fabric for both curtains and skirt was printed in *black* but any other colour may be used.

Registration

1. Spread out the fabric on your printing table and mark off the following distances along both cut edges:
- 4 cm [$1\frac{5}{8}$ in] for an unprinted border
- 38 cm [15 in] for the width of the complete design on Screen 1
- 1 cm [$\frac{3}{8}$ in] for an unprinted strip
- 39 cm [$15\frac{3}{8}$ in] for Screen 2
- 1 cm [$\frac{3}{8}$ in] for an unprinted strip
- 35 cm [$13\frac{3}{4}$ in] for Screen 3
You should be left with an unprinted border of 4 cm [$1\frac{5}{8}$ in].

2. Using a chalk line, join up the marks at either end of the fabric.

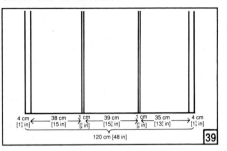

4 cm [$1\frac{5}{8}$ in]   38 cm [15 in]   1 cm [$\frac{3}{8}$ in]   39 cm [$15\frac{3}{8}$ in]   1 cm [$\frac{3}{8}$ in]   35 cm [$13\frac{3}{4}$ in]   4 cm [$1\frac{5}{8}$ in]

120 cm [48 in]   **39**

3. Take Screen 1 (design 8) and place it on the cut edge of the fabric in the 38 cm-wide [15 in-wide] column, lining it up between the chalk lines.
4. Measure the height of the design (it should be 40 cm [$15\frac{3}{4}$ in]) and mark off equivalent distances along the length of the fabric, starting at the top outside edge of the screen. (This is similar to the method used for registering 'Poppies' - see page 73.)
5. Place the screen in its first printing position on the fabric and mark the four places on the frame where the chalk lines intersect it.
6. Similarly, and in their respective columns, mark off along the length of the fabric the height of the designs on Screens 2 and 3. Then register the screens as for Screen 1.

Printing

1. Place Screen 1 in its first printing position, making sure that the four marks on the frame line up with the chalk lines. Begin printing every other space up the column.
2. When you have reached the end of the fabric on the printing table, go back and print the empty spaces.
3. Take Screen 2 and print the central column in the same way.
4. Similarly, take Screen 3 and print the last column.

Finishing

The fabric may be used plain or it may be coloured by sponging or brushing on inks of your choice. Remember to heat-set the printed fabric before and after sponging on additional colour.

Bordered with simple Peruvian-style braids, this fabric also makes striking cushion covers.

CHAPTER FOUR

HAND-CUT FILM STENCILS

Paper stencils start to become limiting as your designs become more complicated. Hand-cut film stencils have the same hard-edged character as paper stencils but there are no loose, moving pieces as there is a backing sheet holding them in place.

Stencil film consists of two layers: a top layer of clear film, parts of which are cut and peeled off to create the desired design (the stencil), and a bottom layer of transparent paper. This bottom layer is not cut through but holds the cut film design in place until it has been bonded to the mesh of the screen. Only then is it peeled off and discarded.

Film stencils also offer other advantages over stencils cut from paper:
The stencil itself is more permanent.
Second and third colours are more easily registered because the stencil is stable.
It is possible to produce and work with very complicated designs.

In your search for new ideas for this medium, page through the books on Japanese and old American stencils. You will see that many of them are just made for the hand-cut film stencil. The ingeniously detailed, clean-cut flower and fish designs of the Japanese are particularly suitable and challenging. Less intricate and demanding, but no less appealing, are the patterns to be found among the stencils applied to the walls of colonial American homes. These designs were inspired mostly by nature – leaves, pineapples and willow trees being especially popular.

(Opposite) Sharp, geometric Ndebele patterns reproduce particularly well when printed with hand-cut film stencils. (Above) Many designs can be successfully scaled down for children's clothing. Alternatively, part of a design can be printed as a feature or highlight, such as the small section of 'Ndebele Border' which was incorporated into the co-ordinated shorts and shirt outfit for this two-year-old.

Stencil Film Materials

Film: available by the metre from screen printing suppliers, it is thinners-based and made specifically for use with water-based textile printing inks.

A stencil cutting knife: ideally as thin as a pencil, it should be comfortable to hold, razor sharp at all times and kept exclusively for cutting film.

Adhering fluid: available from screen printing suppliers who make a special fluid for each type of film they supply - so specify what you require it for.

Cotton rags: old T-shirts are perfect as they are soft, absorbent and do not shed lint on your film.

Degreaser: a special preparation for ensuring a perfectly grease-free mesh, available from screen printing suppliers.

Cutting a Film Stencil

1. Place your drawing or design on a smooth surface and stick the corners down with masking tape. Fill in all the areas to be printed with black ink.

2. Over this place the film. (It should overlap the design by about 5 cm [2 in] all round.) Tape this to the surface as well.

3. Using your cutting knife, 'trace' around the outside edge of each black area, pressing just hard enough on the knife to cut through one layer. (The knife must be held vertically so that the cut film is at right angles to the backing sheet.)

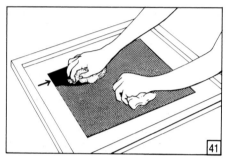

4. With the point of the knife, lift a corner of the cut film and peel it off from all the black areas of your design.

5. Continue in this way, removing the areas to be printed from the top layer of the film until the stencil is complete.

NOTE
Remember that you peel off the film where you want to print, leaving the backing sheet intact.

Bonding a Film Stencil to the Screen

1. It is important to ensure that the screen is completely free of dust and grease, so wash it thoroughly with a proprietary degreaser or a household scouring agent. Then rinse it well and leave it to dry.

2. Lower the screen, underside down, over the cut film so that it is in the centre of the mesh. (There must be perfect contact between mesh and film, so place a 5 mm [¼ in] pile of paper under the film, or a piece of hardboard a few centimetres smaller than the screen.)

3. Pour just enough adhering fluid onto a cotton rag to dampen it. Then, starting in one corner and using even strokes, wipe the rag over the mesh. In your other hand, hold a dry cloth and immediately wipe off any excess fluid.

The object of this procedure is to dissolve the film *just enough to make it sticky*. The film darkens as it becomes wet indicating that it is softening, so do not rub hard or the edges will lose their sharpness - they could even disappear altogether!

4. When the film has stuck, leave it to dry. A fan heater may be used to speed this up, but only on a very low setting.

5. Once dry, turn the screen underside up and peel off the backing sheet. It should come off easily, leaving the film attached to the mesh. (If the film comes off with the backing paper, start Step 3 again.)

6. To block out the area between the film and the frame, pour a small pool of quick-setting proprietary filler onto the screen and pull it over the open mesh with a piece of cardboard. (See the note to Step 7 of 'The Screen' on page 43.) Repeat this process until all four sides of the open mesh have been filled in.

When the filler is dry (about 10 minutes) the screen is ready for printing.

NOTE
Although bonding is not a difficult process, if this is your first film stencil I suggest that you test a small strip of film on the edge of your screen before starting on the completed stencil.

Cleaning the Screen

Lay the screen, squeegee-side up, on a pile of newspaper and pour over enough lacquer thinners to soften the film. Most of the film will stick to the newspaper, the remainder will rub off with a rag moistened with lacquer thinners.

Lining up Designs for Multicolour Printing

When multicolour printing requires the use of more than two screens, it is helpful for all the designs - film stencils or positives for light-sensitive stencils (see final chapter) - to be placed in precisely the same position on each screen. The last project in this chapter ('Kaleidoscope' on page 59) brings us face to face with printing one design in five and then nine colours using five screens. The following method works every time:

1. Find a corner in your workroom that is a true right angle and has a flat work surface fitting into it - a built-in cupboard is best as it cannot move in relation to the wall. Rule a line 10 cm [4 in] away from the wall at the top of the screen and 7.5 cm [3 in] from the wall along the side.

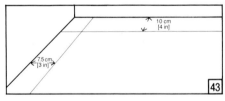

2. Place the main film or positive on the work-top so that its top left- or right-hand corner fits into the drawn right angle. Secure it with masking tape.

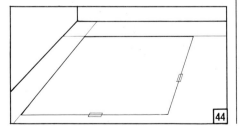

3. Place the second film or positive on top of the first so that it is perfectly registered and put four small blobs of Prestik in the corners, well away from the patterned area.

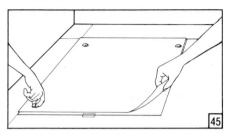

4. Lower a clean or sensitized (see final chapter) screen, underside down, onto the second film or positive, making sure that the frame is touching both walls. Press the mesh down firmly onto the Prestik to ensure that it sticks.

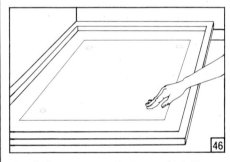

5. Lift the screen with the second film or positive stuck to it and gently set it aside.

6. Without moving the main film or positive, place a small blob of Prestik in each corner and carefully remove the masking tape. Lower the second screen over it, keeping it in contact with the walls, and press the mesh so that the film or positive sticks to it. Then lift it off.

Any number of film stencils or positives for light-sensitive stencils can be lined up in this way, *always leaving the main design until the end*. (This method of lining up screens is not as complicated as it sounds.)

Basic Materials

Screen (61 cm x 56 cm [24 in x 22 in]); squeegee (46 cm [18 in] long); textile printing inks (magenta, azure, primrose, black and clear base); film; stencil cutting knife; masking tape; adhering fluid; cotton rags; proprietary filler or packaging tape; stiff cardboard (about 5 cm x 10 cm [2 in x 4 in] wide); ruler; chalk line.

NDEBELE BORDER

Film stencils are ideal for designs with sharp edges. The designs for this and the next two projects were inspired by the beautiful paintings with which the Ndebele of southern Africa embellish the façades of their dwellings.

Additional Materials
Film: 32.5 cm x 28.5 cm [12$\frac{3}{4}$ in x 11$\frac{1}{4}$ in]
Paint brush: 2.5 cm [1 in] wide (bristle
   length halved)
Pieces of foam sponge
Fabric: own choice
Design: (11) on page 87

The Stencil
1. On a photocopier, enlarge the design until it measures approximately 27.5 cm x 23.5 cm [10$\frac{5}{8}$ in x 9$\frac{1}{4}$ in]. (I did not use rulers and set-squares for this pattern because I thought it would lose its ethnic directness and become geometric and sterile. But because none of the lines are straight, it makes all the measurements approximate.)
2. Tape the design onto a smooth surface, then cut the film 5 cm [2 in] bigger than the design all round and place it over the design. Tape the film down, too.
3. Now cut the stencil following the instructions given on page 50.

The Screen
Follow the instructions given on page 50 for bonding the stencil to the screen.

The Colours
This design looks good printed in a dark blue, then sponged over with turquoise, blue and green. (The precise quantities of

paint required will depend on how much fabric you wish to print.)

1. For the *dark blue*, mix 250 ml [9 fl oz] clear base with 250 ml [9 fl oz] azure, 30 ml [2 tbsp] magenta and 15 ml [1 tbsp] primrose. (I always keep this blue mixed as it is such a good colour for printing.)
2. For the *turquoise*, mix one part azure with four parts clear base.
3. For the *blue*, mix one part navy blue (no. 7 on the colour wheel) with four parts clear base.
4. For the *green*, mix one part green (no. 3 on the colour wheel) with four parts clear base.

Mix all the colours well and test each one on a piece of the same fabric that you will be printing on. Dry each test piece and adjust the colour if necessary.

An alternative colour scheme is black sponged over with stripes of ochre, rust and burgundy. For these dull pastels, try mixing the dull colours with clear base (see page 16).

Registration
1. Mark off 24 cm [9$\frac{1}{2}$ in] lengths along each selvedge (23.5 cm [9$\frac{1}{4}$ in] for the height of the design and 5 mm [$\frac{1}{4}$ in] for the space between the two rows of prints.)
2. With a chalk line, join up the marks across the width of the fabric.
3. *Using 150 cm-wide [59 in-wide] fabric:* five repeats will fit across, leaving 13 cm [5 in] over. Divide this remainder in half and allow for a 6.5 cm [2$\frac{1}{2}$ in] unprinted margin along each selvedge. The torn or cut edges at each end of the fabric should then be marked out as follows:

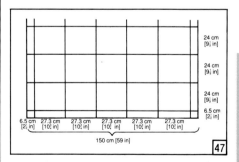

Using 120 cm-wide [48 in-wide] fabric: four repeats will fit across, leaving 10 cm [4 in] over. Allowing for a 5 cm [2 in] un-

— NOTE —
There is an allowance of 2 mm [$\frac{1}{12}$ in] for overlapping the adjacent designs, which is why the marked out width is fractionally less than the repeat.

printed margin along each selvedge and a print overlap of 2 mm [$\frac{1}{12}$ in], mark out your torn or cut edges as follows:

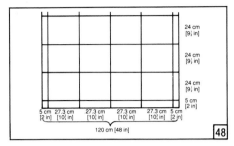

24 cm [9¼ in] · 24 cm [9¼ in] · 24 cm [9¼ in] · 5 cm [2 in]

5 cm [2 in] · 27.3 cm [10¾ in] · 27.3 cm [10¾ in] · 27.3 cm [10¾ in] · 27.3 cm [10¾ in] · 5 cm [2 in]

120 cm [48 in]

48

4. With a chalk line, join up the marks along the length of the fabric.

5. Hold your prepared screen over any one of the central chalk line rectangles. Peering through the mesh, place it so that the lower chalk line runs through the stripe at the bottom of the design on the screen. Now mark the outside edges of the frame exactly where the chalk lines intersect them. (These marks will be your guide to positioning the screen correctly every time you print.)

Printing

1. Working your way across the width of the fabric from one selvedge to the other, print every other rectangle first, then print the ones in between. (If the first prints are not perfectly dry, cover them with strips of newspaper before printing the spaces in between.)

2. In the same way, print alternate rows up the length of the fabric to the end, then return and fill the unprinted rows.

3. Partially heat-set the fabric or leave it to dry thoroughly before painting on additional colours (see page 21).

Sponging on the Colours

When applying fairly wide stripes of additional colour it is quicker to use a sponge than to first paint on the ink and then sponge it.

1. Dilute the turquoise, blue and green inks with water (one part water to three parts printing ink) and stir well.

2. Starting with the first row of designs on the cut edge of the fabric, dip a sponge into the *turquoise* and then wipe it onto the fabric in a stripe. Continue applying ink in this way till you have made a stripe about 10 cm [4 in] wide from selvedge to selvedge. Rub the ink in firmly and evenly so that there are no blobs of excess ink to create patchiness.

3. Using a clean sponge and the *blue* ink, sponge on a 10 cm-wide [4 in-wide] stripe next to the turquoise stripe, allowing it to overlap by about 2 cm [$\frac{3}{4}$ in]. Rub the sponge over the fabric firmly to softly merge the two colours.

4. Now dip a clean sponge into the *green* ink and sponge on a 3 cm-wide [1¼ in-wide] stripe down the centre of the turquoise stripe.

5. Continue this procedure until the entire length of fabric has been sponged.

Finishing

When the inks are dry heat-set the fabric.

This design co-ordinates well with the other Ndebele designs in this chapter. It makes exciting soft furnishings as well as clothes, and it works well as a border or as an all-over design - or a combination of the two.

The impact of 'Ndebele Border' varies according to the colour(s) it is printed in. Strikingly crisp in a single colour on white, the same one-colour print can be livened up by filling in the intricate shapes with jewel-bright silk paints, using a small paint brush.

NDEBELE QUILT

Before creating the design for this project, I had been reading all I could about Turkish tribal rugs. I particularly admired the way the Turks repeat a simple shape or gul (flower) in different colour schemes, arranging them diagonally across a rug. So, starting off with my basic Ndebele shape, which is an enlarged section of the design for 'Ndebele Border' (see page 52), I added Turkish tribal colours and arrangements. I had also noticed that the borders of Turkish rugs echo an element from the main design, and that is what I tried to do on the quilt.

Both this and the next design have many colours, but they are easy to print as each design has a thick black grid which acts as a guide for registration.

Additional Materials
Film: 44 cm [17½ in] square
Brown wrapping paper: 4 pieces 45 cm [17¾ in] square
Fabric (to make a 285 cm x 190 cm [112 in x 75 in] king-size quilt):
  For printing – 6 m x 150 cm-wide [6 yds x 59 in-wide], or 7 m x 120 cm-wide [7¾ yds x 48 in-wide] white calico
  For the backing and trimming – 5.6 m x 120 cm-wide [6¼ yds x 48 in-wide] black cotton or other fabric. (If you have to buy 150 cm-wide [59 in-wide] fabric you will still need 5.6 m [6¼ yds], but you will waste a lot)
  Batting (wadding) – 295 cm x 200 cm [116¼ in x 78¾ in]
Designs: (12) and (13) on pages 88 and 89

PREPARING THE SQUARES

The Film Stencil
1. Using a photocopier, enlarge the design to 39 cm [15¼ in] square. (As the largest piece of paper that a photocopier can accommodate is A3, the design will not fit onto one sheet. It will therefore have to be copied in two parts onto A3 size paper, with a good overlap in the middle, and then glued together so that the design is continuous.)
2. Place the design on a flat surface and tape it down. Cover it with the film (cut 5 cm [2 in] bigger than the design all round) and tape that, too, to the working surface.
3. Cut the stencil according to the instructions on page 50.

The Screen
To prepare the screen for the film stencil, follow the instructions on page 50.

The Fabric
Cut or tear the fabric to give you 24 squares measuring 50 cm x 50 cm [19¾ in x 19¾ in].

Printing
Although it would be possible to print this design on a continuous length of fabric, I prefer to make individual prints on separate fabric squares. This means that I only need to finalise the arrangement of the different squares once they have all been printed.

For printing the design or 'grid' onto the squares, you will need *black* textile printing ink.

1. Spread as many squares on your table as will fit without causing the screen to overlap wet ink while printing on adjacent squares.
2. Take your prepared screen and place it over one of the squares, positioning it as centrally as possible. (The size of the square allows for quite a wide margin of error, so do not worry if the print is slightly off-centre.)
3. Spoon the black ink onto the screen, then pull it over the screen with your squeegee in the usual way.
4. Continue printing the other squares on the table. When you have finished the

first batch, hang them up to dry and spread out more squares.

5. When all 24 fabric squares have been printed, cut four pieces of brown wrapping paper to measure 45 cm [17¾ in] square and make a further print in black ink on each piece.

6. Clean the screen (see page 51).

The next stage is to print the colours. Despite the fact that each square will have four colours, the process is a fairly simple one. You will only need four paper stencils and one extra screen.

The Paper Stencils

In each of the four diagrams opposite, various portions are shaded. Using a stencil craft knife and working with the diagrams as a guide, cut away the shaded sections indicated on the diagrams from the corresponding brown paper prints. Only the areas that have been cut away will then print. (When cutting the paper stencils, remove an extra 3 mm [⅛ in] from around each area so that the ink will overlap the black outline when printing. This allowance is necessary as it is very difficult to register paper stencils perfectly.)

The Screen

To prepare the screen for the paper stencils, mask off the outside edges of a clean screen with packaging tape, leaving free an area 39 cm [15⅜ in] square for printing.

The Colours

Because so many shades of each colour are used in this project, I have not written up a detailed formula for each one. The most important thing to remember when mixing is that none of the colours is straight out of the tub. They must all be mixed with at least 50% clear base and all have small amounts of their complementary colour added (see the instructions for jewel colours on page 15).

1. For the *blues*, mix 300 ml [10½ fl oz] of clear base with 300 ml [10½ fl oz] azure. Divide this quantity between six containers, one for each of the six blues you are going to use. By adding varying proportions of magenta and primrose you will find that you have an amazing

variety of blues. To obtain paler versions of the colours, just add more clear base. (I used turquoise, navy, clear blue, dark turquoise, dark blue and violet.)

With the tip of your finger, smear a little of each colour onto a piece of cotton and leave it to dry. You will be surprised how many shades lighter the inks will dry.

2. For the *reds*, follow the same procedure but start with 200 ml [7 fl oz] magenta and an equal amount of clear base. This will give you a *very* clear, bright pink. Divide this quantity into four containers. Now add a tiny amount each of primrose and azure to tone it down. By adding more azure it will become more maroon and eventually purple. Again, you can vary the darkness of the colour by adding more or less clear base. (The colours I used were pink, maroon, grape and purple.)

3. For the *rust*, take 200 ml [7 fl oz] primrose and add *small* amounts of magenta. (Be very careful as the magenta is much stronger than the yellow and quickly overpowers it, becoming scarlet.) When the colour is a bright orange, add a tiny quantity of azure to turn it into rust.

4. For the *brown* and *ochre*, add 100 ml [3½ fl oz] of primrose to an equal quantity of clear base, then add minute amounts of magenta and azure. Now add a tiny bit of black. (These are the only colours to which I add black.)

5. For the *acid greens*, start with 50 ml [10 tsp] each of primrose and clear base, then carefully add very small amounts of blue and red until you arrive at the correct colour.

6. For the *pale green*, start with 45 ml [3 tbsp] clear base and add a small quantity of blue and an even smaller amount of magenta and primrose.

Preparing for Printing

1. To simplify the colour printing, look at diagram 53 in the adjacent column which illustrates the layout of the quilt. Each number represents one of nine colour schemes (explained in the chart in Step 2). It also indicates how many squares will be printed in each colour scheme.

Now, using a fabric marking pen, mark your printed fabric squares in precisely the same way. In other words, there will

53			
1	2	3	4
2	3	4	5
3	4	5	6
4	5	6	7
5	6	7	8
6	7	8	9

be one square marked '1' and one marked '9'; two squares marked '2' and two squares marked '8', and so on.

2. All the squares are printed four times, many with a different arrangement of colours. The following chart shows you how many squares will be printed in which colour and with which stencil.

Numbered squares (see diag. 53)	No. of squares (to be printed)	Stencil 1 (diag. 49)	Stencil 2 (diag. 50)	Stencil 3 (diag. 51)	Stencil 4 (diag. 52)
1	1	beige	turquoise	navy	blue
2	2	rust	blue	navy	beige
3	3	pink	maroon	navy	blue
4	4	olive	blue	dark turq.	dark blue
5	4	rust	dark blue	violet	navy
6	4	pink	maroon	grape	pale green
7	3	brown	turquoise	dark turq.	beige
8	2	pink	maroon	purple	dark turq.
9	1	olive	grape	violet	pink

Take, as an example, the fabric square which you have marked '1' as in diagram 53. Working across the chart, you will see that fabric square '1' is the only square to be printed in beige by the first stencil, turquoise by the second stencil, navy by the third stencil and blue by the fourth. No other square will be printed with that colour configuration. Similarly, only two squares will be printed with the colour scheme for those squares marked with a '2' (rust, blue, navy and beige).

Printing

1. Align the *first stencil* (diagram 49) with the fabric square marked '1'. By looking through the cut-out part of the stencil you will be able to see the area you are going to print, as well as a small (3 mm [⅛ in]) amount of the black printed line on the fabric where the colour will overlap. Lower the screen, underside down, over the paper stencil, checking through the mesh that the paper has not moved.

2. Spoon the *beige* ink onto the screen and print the square marked '1'.

3. Remove the screen (the ink will have stuck the paper to the mesh), scrape up the remaining beige ink with a piece of cardboard and return it to its container.

4. The next colour to be printed with the first stencil is *pink*. This will be printed onto the squares marked '3', '6' and '8' - a total of nine squares.

First, make a trial print on a piece of newspaper to ensure that no trace of beige is printing. Then lower the screen onto each square in turn, registering by looking through the mesh at the black grid of the printed design. When all nine squares have been printed, scoop out the remaining ink with a clean piece of cardboard and return it to its container.

5. Next, print the *olive* onto the four squares marked '4' and the one marked '9'.

6. Now print the *brown* onto the three squares marked '7'.

7. The final prints with the first stencil are in *rust*. Print the two squares marked '2' and the four squares marked '5'.

—— NOTE ——
The reason why the squares are not printed in the logical order of 1- 9 is that if you work through the colours from pale to dark it should not be necessary to wash the whole screen until all the printing from the one stencil has been completed.

8. Pull off the paper stencil and clean the screen with a strong jet of water.

9. When the screen and the ink on the squares are dry, look down the second column of colours in the above chart and select the inks for printing the *second stencil* (diagram 50). It is best to print the *maroon* (nine squares) first, then the *grape* (one square), then print the different *blues* (including the *turquoise*), starting with the palest.

10. Remove the stencil and clean the screen. Then, using the *third stencil* (diagram 51), start printing with *grape*, followed by *violet*, then *purple* and lastly the *blues*.

11. Finally, take the *fourth stencil* (diagram 52) and print the *beige*, followed by *pale green*, *pink*, and lastly the *blues*.

When all the squares have been printed, lay them in order on the floor. If you are not happy with any of the colours, over-print them.

PREPARING THE BORDER

The Film Stencil
1. Enlarge design (11) so that it measures 31 cm x 14 cm [12¼ in x 5½ in].
2. Cut the stencil film following the instructions given on page 50.

The Screen

Bond the film to the screen following the instructions given on page 50.

The Colours

1. You will need *black* for printing the basic design.

2. For the *turquoise*, mix one part azure with two parts clear base, then add a tiny amount of orange (no. 11 on the colour wheel).

3. For the *blue,* mix one part azure with two parts clear base and add magenta, teaspoon by teaspoon, until the right colour is achieved.

4. For the *maroon,* mix one part magenta with two parts clear base and add a speck of green (no. 3 on the colour wheel) to tone down the brightness.

The Fabric

1. Cut or tear the fabric to give you:
Two strips measuring 290 cm x 20 cm [114 in x 8 in]
Two strips measuring 175 cm x 20 cm [69 in x 8 in]

2. Spread the strips of fabric on your printing table and smooth them out.

Registration

Make a chalk line 3 cm [$1\frac{1}{4}$ in] up from the lower edge of the strip; alternatively, use a long plank of wood to guide the screen when you begin printing (see 'Registration: method 2' on page 17).

The Black Outline

1. Following the same procedure as used for printing the green border for 'Hawaiian Quilt' (see page 27), spoon black ink onto the screen and print the two long borders with 10 repeats each and the two shorter borders with six repeats each. (Overlap each print by 2 mm [$\frac{1}{12}$ in].)

2. Print one border design on a piece of brown paper for use as a stencil, then clean the screen thoroughly with a strong jet of water.

The Paper Stencil

Take the brown paper on which the bor-

— NOTE —
The strips are a little longer than necessary but they will be trimmed to the correct length once the squares have been joined.

der design has been printed and you will see that there are three stepped shapes opposite the striped line.

Using a craft knife, cut out these pieces so that there is a good overlap of colour onto the black. Remove about 5 mm [$\frac{1}{4}$ in] of the black line surrounding each of these areas. (Paper stencils are not at all accurate so a large overlap is necessary.)

The Screen

Using an HB pencil, draw a rectangle 31 cm x 14 cm [$12\frac{1}{4}$ in x $5\frac{1}{2}$ in] on a clean screen. Block off the surrounding area with packaging tape.

Printing

1. Place the paper stencil on the printed border, lining up the cut-out areas with the printed pattern beneath.

2. Taking care not to displace the stencil, lower the screen so that the taped rectangle on the screen lines up with the stencil (visible through the mesh). Print the design in *turquoise* and continue until all the turquoise has been printed on all four borders.

3. Do not wash the screen, simply scrape the ink off the mesh and the squeegee with a piece of cardboard. Turn the screen around 180° and you will find that it fits over the other row of stepped shapes as well. Print these in *blue*.

4. Scrape the ink off the screen and the squeegee as before. Discard the paper stencil and wash the screen thoroughly.

5. Block off the whole screen with paper or tape, except for a 40 cm x 3 cm [$15\frac{3}{4}$ in x $1\frac{1}{4}$ in] strip. Now print the *maroon* stripes. It is easy to register them by looking through the mesh.

When you have completed all the printing and the ink is dry, heat-set the fabric.

This border was designed specifically for the 'Ndebele Quilt', but it is also useful for the bottoms of skirts, the yokes of shirts, and collars. The colours can be printed with a paper stencil or just filled in with a paint brush and textile printing inks.

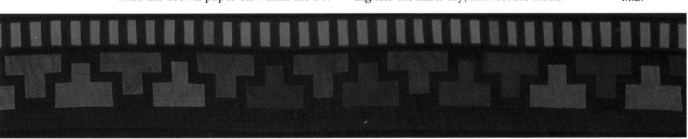

TO ASSEMBLE THE QUILT

1. Trim the white border around each printed square to 1.5 cm [⅝ in].

2. Lay all the squares on the floor and decide on the final sequence of colours.

3. Sew the top row of four squares together, carefully matching the corners and edges, then sew together the other five rows of four squares so that you have six strips altogether.

4. Press the seam allowance of all the squares to one side, then join the strips together.

5. Overlock or zig-zag all those edges that may fray.

6. Sew on the short borders first and press them well, then join on the two long borders so that they overlap the short borders.

7. Cut and sew the backing fabric to make a rectangle measuring 295 cm x 200 cm [117 in x 79 in]. The excess will be trimmed off after quilting.

8. Place your backing fabric, wrong side up, on the floor and spread the batting (wadding) over it. (Do not join or overlap the batting in order to make a single rectangle as a join will make a bulky ridge in the quilt. Simply butt the edges where two pieces need to be joined and hold them in place with a few temporary stitches. They will be held in place later by the quilting.) Now place the pieced front, right side up, on top of the batting (wadding).

9. Tack the three layers together, beginning in the centre and working towards the corners and sides. The more you tack the easier it will be to machine quilt as the three layers will not move in relation to each other and pucker up.

10. Machine quilt in all the grooves of the seams between the squares, again beginning in the centre of the quilt and working towards the corners and sides.

11. To make the edge trim, measure the width of the quilt and cut two pieces of black fabric to that measurement by 12 cm [5 in] wide.

12. Measure the length of the quilt, including the width of the edge trim for the top and bottom, and cut two pieces the same length, both with a width of 12 cm [5 in].

13. With right sides facing, sew the top and bottom edge trim to the quilt. Then fold the trim back, turn it under and hand hem to the backing fabric.

14. Repeat with the two long edges, overlapping the trim on the short edges. Turn the edge trim to the back and hand hem to the backing fabric.

The colour scheme given is only a suggestion. Why not try your own combination of colours to match a special room in your house?

NOTE
The size of the quilt can easily be adjusted to suit any bed size. Extra squares can be added to the width, or more borders can be added.

Although the design for this quilt was Ndebele-inspired, the colours have their origins in the rich dyes of Turkish and Persian rugs.

KALEIDOSCOPE

As this design has four colours printed over it, it is ideal to work with five screens.* If, however, you do not have five screens, it is perfectly possible to achieve the same result with two: one for the black framework, using a film stencil, and one for the other colours, using paper stencils, as in the previous project.**

Instructions for printing this design are given first for its use as a border (see the jacket on page 6) and then as an all-over design (see opposite the title page where it features as a cushion cover).

Additional Materials
* 4 additional screens
    1 m of film (this allows for five separate stencils to be cut, with a 5 cm [2 in] space around each design)
**1 additional screen
    piece of film measuring 41 cm x 31 cm [16 in x $12\frac{1}{4}$ in]
Brown wrapping paper
Fabric: own choice
Design: (14) on page 89

AS A BORDER

The Film Stencils
1. Cut your film into five separate sheets, allowing a border of 5 cm [2 in] around each design.
2. Enlarge the design so that it measures 35.2 cm x 25.3 cm [$13\frac{7}{8}$ in x 10 in].
3. Cut out the stencil following the instructions on page 50 but leave it in position over the design.

4. Lay the second sheet of film on top of the first and cut out all the areas indicated in diagram 55. Make sure that the cutting line runs down the centre of the black lines so that the colour will overlap the black by about 2 mm [$\frac{1}{12}$ in] when printed.
5. Remove the second piece of film and repeat the procedure following diagrams 56, 57 and 58 as colour guides, each time leaving only the first piece of film in position over the design.

The Screens
1. Wash and degrease the screens.
2. Line up the stencils with the screens, following the instructions on page 51.
3. Bond the film to the screens, following the instructions on page 50 and number the screens from 1 to 5.

The Fabric
Cut or tear a strip of fabric 35 cm [14 in] wide (the length of the strip will depend on what you want to make), then smooth out the fabric on the printing table.

Registration
Mark the entire length of the strip with a chalk line 5 cm [2 in] up from the lower edge. Follow the instructions for registering a border given in the 'Hawaiian Quilt' project on page 28. (The repeat is 35 cm [$13\frac{4}{5}$ in], which includes an allowance for a 2 mm [$\frac{1}{12}$ in] overlap.)

The Colours
1. You will need *black* for the basic design.
2. For the *turquoise*, mix 250 ml [9 fl oz] clear base with 30 ml [2 tbsp] azure and 7.5 ml [$1\frac{1}{2}$ tsp] primrose.
3. For the *pale turquoise*, mix 250 ml [9 fl oz] clear base with 30 ml [2 tbsp] of mixed turquoise.
4. For the *indigo blue*, mix 125 ml [$4\frac{1}{2}$ fl oz] clear base with 125 ml [$4\frac{1}{2}$ fl oz] azure, 15 ml [1 tbsp] magenta and 15 ml [1 tbsp] primrose.
5. For the *green*, mix the same ingredients for making turquoise, then add primrose 2.5 ml [$\frac{1}{2}$ tsp] at a time until the right green is reached.

Test all the colours on a piece of the fabric you will be printing onto and adjust them if and where necessary.

> **— NOTE —**
> Any transparent colour printed on black does not show, so it is perfectly safe to have a generous overlap.

55

56

57

58

Registration

1. Place the screen for the black design on the left-hand side of the fabric so that you can see the chalk line through the bottom line of the stencil. Mark the frame where the chalk line intersects it.

2. The width of the design is 35.2 cm [14 in] and you will need a 2 mm [$\frac{1}{12}$ in] overlap. So, from the outer edge of the screen, mark off 35 cm [13$\frac{3}{4}$ in] lengths as illustrated in diagram 5 on page 17.

Printing

1. Print alternate sections following the method used for printing the 'Hawaiian Quilt' borders (see page 28). Now the framework of the border is printed and it is simply a matter of filling in the colours.

2. Take the *second prepared screen* and, following the same procedure as for Step 1 above, print in *turquoise* the area indicated in diagram 55.

3. Similarly, print the *third screen* in *pale turquoise* as indicated in diagram 56, the *fourth screen* in *indigo blue* as indicated in diagram 57 and the *fifth screen* in *green* as indicated in diagram 58.

The border is now ready to be heat-set.

NOTE
It is very easy to line up the screen on the black printed design.

AS AN ALL-OVER PRINT

Do you feel ready to try an all-over nine-colour print? If you completed the border successfully, you will easily manage this as it is just a series of borders printed one after the other in alternating colourways.

The Screens

Use the same screens as you used for printing the border or, if you are printing this design for the first time, follow the directions given for preparing the stencils and screens for the border.

Registration

1. Mark out 26.8 cm [10$\frac{5}{8}$ in] lengths along both selvedges and join the corresponding marks from selvedge to selvedge with a chalk line. (The 26.8 cm [10$\frac{5}{8}$ in] includes 25.3 cm [10 in] for the height of the black printed design and 1.5 cm [$\frac{5}{8}$ in] for the space between each row of designs. This space is printed by Screen 3 in plum and scarlet alternately.)

2. *Using 150 cm-wide [59 in-wide] fabric:* four repeats 35 cm [13$\frac{3}{4}$ in] wide (this includes an allowance of 2 mm [$\frac{1}{12}$ in] for an overlap) will fit across leaving 10 cm [4 in] over. Divide the 10 cm [4 in] in half and allow for a 5 cm [2 in] unprinted strip along each selvedge.

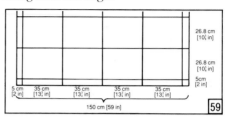

Using 120 cm-wide [48 in-wide] fabric: three repeats will fit across, leaving 15 cm [6 in] over. Divide this in half and allow for a 7.5 cm [3 in] unprinted strip along each selvedge.

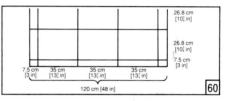

3. Mark off the repeats along the cut ends of the fabric and join them with a chalk line (see diagrams 58 and 59).

The Colours

1. You will need *black* to print the basic design (Screen 1).

2. For the *deep red*, mix 150 ml [5 fl oz] clear base, with 60 ml [4 tbsp] magenta, 5 ml [1 tsp] azure and 5 ml [1 tsp] primrose.

3. For the *plum*, mix 150 ml [5 fl oz] clear base with 60 ml [4 tbsp] magenta, 7.5 ml [1$\frac{1}{2}$ tsp] azure and 2.5 ml [$\frac{1}{2}$ tsp] primrose.

4. For the *pale plum*, mix 150 ml [5 fl oz] clear base with 30 ml [2 tbsp] magenta, 3.25 ml [$\frac{3}{4}$ tsp] azure and 1.25 ml [$\frac{1}{4}$ tsp] primrose.

5. For the *bright pink*, mix 150 ml [5 fl oz] clear base with 30 ml [2 tbsp] magenta and 1.25 ml [$\frac{1}{4}$ tsp] each of azure and primrose.

6. For the *scarlet*, mix 150 ml [5 fl oz] clear base with 60 ml [4 tbsp] magenta, 1.25 ml [$\frac{1}{4}$ tsp] azure and 15 ml [1 tbsp] primrose.

7. For the *pale apricot*, mix 150 ml [5 fl oz] clear base with 2.5 ml [$\frac{1}{2}$ tsp] magenta, 1.25 ml [$\frac{1}{4}$ tsp] azure and 5 ml [1 tsp] primrose.

The strong designs and colours of 'Kaleidoscope' on the jacket, combined with 'Ndebele Border' as an all-over print for the skirt, result in an eye-catching ensemble for all occasions.

8. For the *clear blue*, mix 150 ml [5 floz] clear base with 30 ml [2 tbsp] azure and 1.25 ml [$\frac{1}{4}$ tsp] magenta.

9. For the *indigo*, mix 150 ml [5 fl oz] clear base with 30 ml [2 tbsp] azure, 10 ml [2 tsp] magenta and 10 ml [2 tsp] primrose.

Printing

Once the basic design (Screen 1) has been printed, the colours are printed according to the scheme set out below:

Screen	Stencil cut from	Odd rows	Even rows
2	diag. 54	deep red	bright pink
3	diag. 55	plum	scarlet
4	diag. 56	clear blue	indigo
5	diag. 57	pale plum	pale apricot

1. Take the *first screen* (basic design) and place it on any of the rectangles marked out on the fabric. (The blue chalk line must just be visible on the lower edge of the bottom line of the design.) You will see that two chalk lines cross under each

side of the screen. Mark these eight points on the outside of the frame to assist you in registering the screen when the ink prevents you seeing through the mesh (see page 18 for instructions for registering an all-over design).

2. Starting from the left-hand edge of the first row, and working systematically across the fabric, print every alternate block in *black*, then return to your starting point and print the spaces. (Before filling in a space, do remember to check that the ink in the adjacent blocks is dry. If it is not, shield those areas with pieces of newspaper to prevent your screen transferring unwanted ink.)

3. When the fabric on the table has been printed in black, clean the ink from the screen and leave the fabric to dry.

4. Take the *second screen* and place it over any centrally positioned print. Line up the area which is to be printed in *deep red* with the black printed 'grid' on the fabric. Mark the frame at the eight points where the chalk lines intersect.

5. Place the screen on the first repeat to be printed and, using the deep red ink, print a whole row.

6. Miss the second row and print the third.

7. Continue printing alternate rows until you come to the end of the fabric. (This will depend on the length of the table and how much fabric you are printing. I prefer to print a table length of fabric in black ink and then print the colours before moving the fabric on.)

8. Scrape the ink from the screen and the squeegee with a piece of cardboard. Next, spoon the *bright pink* ink onto the screen. Make one print on a piece of newspaper to clear away the last of the old colour, then print all the even rows.

9. Take the *third screen* and print the first and every alternate row with *plum* ink, and the even rows with *scarlet*.

10. Taking the *fourth screen*, print first in *clear blue* and then in *indigo*.

11. Taking the *fifth screen*, print first in *pale plum* and finally in *pale apricot*.

Finishing

When the inks are dry, heat-set the fabric.

This nine-colour print is a lot of work and takes a long time to complete, but it is very satisfying - and worth the effort!

NOTE When printing more than one colour it is better not to move the fabric until all the colours have been printed. This design, however, has a wide black 'grid' to absorb mistakes, so it is not too critical if the fabric has to be moved.

CHAPTER FIVE

LIGHT-SENSITIVE STENCILS

In the foregoing chapters, each of the stencils you have experimented with has imparted its own distinctive characteristics to the prints: paper stencils produce simple designs which are clear-cut with sharp, clean edges; painted screens transfer a softer, more painterly quality to the printed design, while film stencils, though sharing the characteristics of paper stencils, make possible far more complicated designs. Light-sensitive stencils, however, do not have a distinctly individual quality.

By using a simple photographic technique, it is possible for a screen to reproduce on fabric the characteristics of any of the graphic arts - from pen and pencil drawings to lithographs and etchings. To achieve this, a light-sensitive emulsion is applied to the screen. An opaque design is then placed on top of the screen to prevent light reaching the emulsion and the screen is exposed to ultra-violet light (the sun or a mercury vapour lamp). To produce a stencil from the exposed emulsion, the screen is washed with a strong jet of water. Those parts of the emulsion which were covered by the positive will wash away as they remain water-soluble, while those parts which were exposed to the light will have hardened to form the stencil.

The opaque design, or 'positive transparency', is normally drawn with black ink onto architectural tracing paper, although anything that is flat and opaque can be used, including grasses, leaves, black lace or paper.

All commercial screen printers use light-sensitive stencils. They are precise, easy to apply and versatile. Also, they can be kept for many years and are capable of making thousands of prints without any deterioration in quality.

(Opposite) This delightful design comprises 20 different guineafowl. To avoid drawing by hand the 120 guineafowl required to fill a screen, the design can be reproduced directly onto light-sensitive mesh (see page 70). (Above) From high fashion (page 6) and youthful charm (page 7) to practical home décor, as in this Roman blind, the 'Butterflies' design manifests its versatility in black and white.

Additional Materials

FOR PREPARING THE SCREEN

Light-sensitive emulsion: Autosol WR or Dirasol Photostencil System (Sericol) - available in 1 kg [2 lb 2 oz] packs and sufficient for coating at least twenty 61 cm x 56 cm [24 in x 22 in] screens.

Trough: similar in appearance to a piece of aluminium guttering, it is used for applying the emulsion and is available from screen printing suppliers.

Roughening paste: (Autoprep) a thick, grey abrasive paste, used for roughening the mesh before applying the light-sensitive emulsion.

Degreasing agent: (Universal Mesh Prep) necessary for cleaning the screen (a household product will not serve the purpose).

Decoating solution: (Autostrip Gel) a chemical preparation for removing the stencil from the screen.

Fan heater: useful for speeding up the drying process after the screen has been washed and coated with emulsion.

FOR PREPARING THE POSITIVE

Architectural tracing paper: necessary for tracing designs.

Drawing pen: for lines of an even thickness, a draughting pen is ideal (Rotring or Faber Castell with a .7 mm [$\frac{1}{30}$ in] nib), otherwise an ordinary dip-pen can be used to create more interesting lines.

Water colour brush: a good quality sable or imitation sable brush (about a size 3), necessary for painting designs onto tracing paper or filling in outlines.

Black ink: Rotring FL - highly recommended because it is very opaque (eliminating the need for a repeat layer) and very fluid - may be applied with a pen or watercolour brush.

> —— NOTE ——
> Anything that produces an opaque line or an opaque filled-in area can be used instead of Rotring FL ink. Try black oil pastel, a 4B pencil or black spray paint. Indian ink works well, too, but never use it with a mechanical/draughting pen as it will clog the pen permanently. (Felt-tip pens are not sufficiently opaque, nor is fountain pen ink.)

FOR EXPOSING THE SCREEN USING THE SUN

Sheet of glass: cut to the size of the screen (stick masking tape around the edges so that you do not cut your hand).

FOR EXPOSING THE SCREEN USING A LAMP

Exposure box with mercury vapour lamp: Think twice before rushing out to buy an exposure box (see page 66). I prefer using sunlight whenever possible as it unquestionably results in a more evenly developed stencil. The sun does not always shine, though, and if you only work with the occasional light-sensitive stencil or feel hesitant about the whole thing, it would be better, initially, to ask your stockist or local screen printer to expose your screen for you. Ask if you can watch the exposure process; maybe then you will feel braver about doing it yourself.

Preparing the Screen

ROUGHENING AND DEGREASING THE SCREEN

The monofilaments that make up the warp and weft of the mesh are very smooth, so to make it easier for the emulsion to adhere it is necessary to roughen them. This is done with a commercial roughening paste (Autoprep). The procedure is best carried out out-of-doors.

1. Wet both sides of the screen, scrape up some Autoprep with the bristles of a dish-washing or scrubbing brush and rub it into both sides of the mesh, using a circular motion.

2. Leave the screen to stand for 2 to 5 minutes, then hose it off, removing every last trace of abrasive.

Next, the mesh must be degreased so that the emulsion will stick.

1. Wet the mesh and pour 15 ml [1 tbsp] of degreaser onto one side of the mesh. Rub it over the entire surface with a dish-washing brush. Repeat on the other side.

2. Let the screen stand for 2 to 5 minutes, then hose it off and leave it to dry.

> —— NOTE ——
> Never be tempted to leave out the roughening and degreasing procedure, no matter how well you cleaned your screen when it was last used. I have - and regretted it. The emulsion is likely to develop pinholes or wash out where you do not want it to.
>
> Do not touch the mesh after these cleaning preparations, as fingerprints can leave a greasy mark.

Cover the screen with a sheet of plastic or paper until you are ready to apply the emulsion. (It is preferable to prepare the screen on the same day that the emulsion is going to be applied - or the day before at the earliest - as dust settling on the mesh can cause pinholes in the stencil.)

SENSITIZING THE SCREEN

A darkroom is not necessary for working with light-sensitive emulsion. During the day just draw the curtains. (If the light is still very strong, pin or peg a blanket from the curtain rail.) At night, turn off the lights in your workroom and open a door to let in the light from an adjacent room or passage.

Light-sensitive emulsion comes in a pack comprising a small bucket of thick viscous liquid and a tiny plastic bottle containing the light-sensitive chemical. Add warm water to the small bottle to three-quarter fill it and shake until the dark liquid is well combined with the water. Add this to the bucket and mix well. Once mixed, the emulsion has a *refrigerated* shelf-life of three months.

1. Stir the emulsion with a plastic or wooden stick each time before using it, then pour it along the length of the trough. (Do not fill the trough as only a small amount of emulsion is needed - approximately 100 ml [$3\frac{1}{2}$ fl oz]).

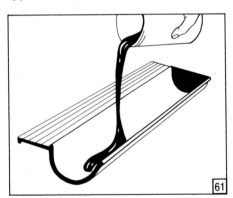

2. Hold the screen on its edge with one hand and angle it away from you. (It does not matter which side of the screen is facing out as both sides will need to be coated.) With the other hand, hold the trough against the lower edge of the mesh, just above the frame. Next, pressing the trough quite firmly against the mesh, tip it so that the emulsion runs to the very edge and along the full length of

the trough. Now move the trough slowly and firmly up the mesh, so that an even layer of emulsion is deposited.

3. Apply two coats of emulsion to each side of the screen - wet on wet.
4. Return any unused emulsion to the container as it can be reused.
5. Leave the screen to dry in a horizontal position, underside down.

The screen is now light-sensitive and it is best to expose it as soon as possible. If you cannot do so straight away, store it in a black plastic bag in a cool place. (I have stored a screen in this way for a week without any resulting problems.)

---**NOTE**---
You can use a fan heater to speed up the drying process but the heat must not exceed 30 ˚C.
Most commercial printers offer the service of coating a screen, as well as exposing it.

Exposing the Screen
Whichever method of exposure you use - the sun or a lamp - the principle of exposure remains the same.

EXPOSURE BY THE SUN
Working in a room with the curtains drawn:
1. Turn the screen, squeegee-side down, onto a piece of hardboard which has been completely covered with a large, dark cloth. This is to prevent any light reflecting onto the squeegee side of the screen when it is carried outside.)
2. On the sensitized underside of the

screen, arrange leaves, grass, drawing, positive transparency or other positive.

3. To ensure closer contact with the emulsion, place a sheet of clean glass over everything. (If the positive is not pressed flat, the edges of the printed shapes will be fuzzy.)

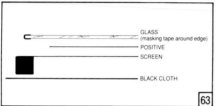

GLASS (masking tape around edge)
POSITIVE
SCREEN
BLACK CLOTH

63

4. Take the screen, with the non-reflective surface underneath, out into the sunlight and leave it there for 2 to 5 minutes. (The strength of the sun is so variable that you will have to experiment with exposure times.)

5. When sufficiently exposed, take the screen out of the sun and remove the glass and the positive. (You will see that the areas exposed to the light are a slightly different colour.)

> **NOTE**
> Start timing as soon as you walk out into the sunlight and include the time it takes to walk back inside.

> **NOTE**
> The instructions on your emulsion pack will not specify times for exposing a screen in sunlight - it will just give maximum and minimum times. These times will vary according to the speed of the emulsion you are using.
>
> Strong sunlight gives the same strength of exposure as a mercury vapour lamp.
>
> Fine lines tend to close up if they are exposed for too long, so they need the minimum exposure time.
>
> Large, solid positives require the maximum exposure.

EXPOSURE BY A MERCURY VAPOUR LAMP

There are many ultra-violet lamps: some work better than others. I can, however, recommend the Philips 125W High Pressure Mercury Vapour Repro Lamp (HPMVR), available from screen printing suppliers. It is expensive but reliable. Sun lamps, too, can be used, although the exposure time will be longer, but if you already have one it definitely would be worth experimenting with it.

If you are using a mercury vapour lamp, you will need an exposure box. This can be purchased from screen printing suppliers. It is also very easy to make from pine, hardboard and glass.

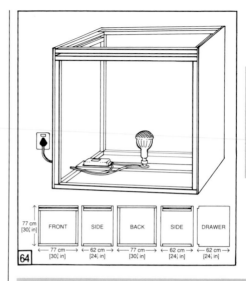

77 cm [30¼ in]

FRONT | SIDE | BACK | SIDE | DRAWER
77 cm [30¼ in] | 62 cm [24¼ in] | 77 cm [30¼ in] | 62 cm [24¼ in] | 62 cm [24¼ in]

64

> **NOTE**
> The front panel of the box has been removed to show the inside. The top is covered by a sheet of glass.

> **NOTE**
> If you are working during the daytime your room will be sufficiently dark if you just close the curtains. At night, turn off the light in your workroom and leave the door open to let in light from an adjacent room or passage.
>
> The instructions that are enclosed with the light-sensitive emulsion pack sound formidable but the manufacturers are really just 'playing safe'. As long as no direct light falls onto the light-sensitive emulsion you should have no problems.

1. Place the positive(s) on the glass top of the box.

2. Over this, place the screen, squeegee-side up, covered with a dark, non-reflective material (it can be a black plastic bag) to prevent reflected light from exposing the screen from above.

3. To ensure maximum contact between positive and mesh, place a thin sheet of foam rubber (cut to fit just inside the frame) over the dark material, followed by a similar size sheet of hardboard; then weigh the layers down with four bricks.

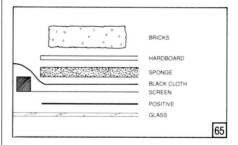

BRICKS
HARDBOARD
SPONGE
BLACK CLOTH
SCREEN
POSITIVE
GLASS

65

4. Switch on the lamp and wait for about 2 minutes for the light to reach full strength, then pull out the sliding shelf beneath the glass top and start timing the exposure. (See pages 65 to 66 for notes on exposure.)

5. Replace the shelf and turn off the lamp, but if there are more screens to expose, keep it burning as turning the lamp on and off too frequently reduces its life.

6. Put the screen in a black plastic bag to take to the bathroom, or wherever you intend washing it out.

Washing out the Screen

1. Using an adjustable spray nozzle, or just your thumb over the end of a hose-pipe to create a pressurised spray, hose the screen gently on both sides. The part of the screen which was covered by the positive (the non-exposed part) will become paler and start washing away.

2. Increase the pressure to wash out these pale areas completely, then hold the screen up to the window to make sure that the printing areas on the mesh are absolutely clear.

NOTE

If the parts of the stencil that were covered with opaque designs do not wash out, the screen was over-exposed. To correct this, reduce the length of exposure time when you next expose the screen.

If exposed parts wash away, either the screen has been under-exposed, or the emulsion is too old, or the mesh was not properly prepared.

---

3. To remove any remaining unexposed emulsion which can run into the printing areas, carefully blot the mesh with a single sheet of newspaper - a clean piece for each side. (Do not move the paper around on the screen or you may transfer dissolved emulsion to a printing area.)

4. To dry and further strengthen the exposed emulsion, take the screen into the sun or place it in a warm, dry spot indoors for about half an hour.

5. Now fill in the area between the emulsion and the frame using either packaging tape, a proprietary filler (as used for film-cut stencils), or a further coating of light-sensitive emulsion which, after drying, will require exposing as above.

Cleaning the Screen

As it is necessary to use a special decoating chemical to remove the exposed emulsion, it is advisable to carry out this cleaning operation outside. *The use of rubber gloves is essential.* I also wear a mask as the toxic fumes are quite potent.

1. Using a dish-washing or scrubbing brush with a handle, apply a thin layer of decoating solution to each side of the screen and leave it for 5 minutes - or longer if the stencil has been on for a long time. *Do not allow it to dry completely as it will form an impervious film.*

2. Spray the screen with water and the stencil will wash off.

If there are still bits of film and ink adhering to the screen, a strong solvent, such as Autosolve, can be used with a potent cleansing paste (Autopaste). Another good cleaner is Universal Stain Cleaner. This is the procedure:

1. Put the screen, underside down, on newspaper and pour on enough Autosolve to wet the screen. Let it soak for a few minutes.

2. Using a stiff dish-washing brush, scoop up enough cleansing paste to thinly cover each side and work it into the screen on both sides.

3. Leave the screen for 5 minutes, then hose it off with water.

Alternatively, if you dislike handling chemicals, you can take your screen to your supplier who will remove the photographic stencil for a small charge.

Basic Materials

Sensitized screen 61 cm x 56 cm [24 in x 22 in]; squeegee 46 cm [18 in] long; textile printing inks (magenta, azure, primrose, black and clear base); ruler or tape measure; light-sensitive emulsion; trough 46 cm [18 in] long; roughening paste; degreaser; dark non-reflective cloth; black plastic bag; filler or packaging tape; decoating solution; craft knife; cutting board; HB pencil; ruler; chalk line; fabric marking pen.

For exposing by sunlight, you will need, in addition, a piece of glass measuring 61 cm x 56 cm [24 in x 22 in].

For exposing by mercury vapour lamp, you will need, in addition, an exposure box fitted with a mercury vapour lamp, a piece of foam and two bricks.

GRASSES

NOTE

Some grasses are very translucent. To effectively block the sun from the light-sensitive emulsion, spray them with a dark paint.

This is a wonderful project to do with children of any age, as it demonstrates so clearly the different shapes and sizes of leaves and grasses which they can find in their own environment.

Additional Materials

Fabric: own choice
Grasses and leaves of as many different shapes as possible

If you work on this project with children, it is more suitable to use the sun to expose the emulsion because it is part of nature, as are the leaves and grasses. If this is not possible, however, then of course use a mercury vapour lamp.

The Stencil

1. Spread a black plastic bag on a table and place the screen on top, squeegee-side down.
2. Arrange the grasses and leaves on the sensitized mesh.
3. Place a sheet of glass on top.
4. Carry the screen outside into the sunlight and leave it there for a $\frac{1}{2}$ to 1 minute - longer if it is not the middle of the day.
5. Bring the screen inside, remove the grasses and leaves, then wash out the emulsion with a hose, spraying harder as the image of the grasses and leaves ap-

NOTE

Remember to start timing the moment you step outside.

pears (see page 67 for full instructions).
6. Blot the screen with newspaper and leave to dry.
7. Cover the area between the emulsion and the frame with filler and you are ready to print.

The Colours

Inspired by a bunch of dried flowers bought at a craft market, I used an unusual peachy pink as the main colour, complementing it with beiges and browns. By using the same screen and overprinting many times in different colours, a wonderful fullness is achieved.

1. For the *pink*, add 5 ml [1 tsp] of magenta to 250 ml [9 fl oz] clear base and mix well, then add tiny amounts of primrose, testing it after each addition. When you feel it is right, dry it to be sure.
2. For the *brown*, add 5 ml [1 tsp] each of magenta, black and primrose to 250 ml [9 fl oz] clear base.
3. For the *beige*, combine equal quantities of brown and clear base.

The Fabric

Spread out the fabric on your printing table. (Unless a perfectly regular print is required, it is not necessary to mark out registration lines.)

Printing

The grasses can be printed as a border or as an all-over print. As no registration is necessary, simply print where you think they will look good.

1. Working across the fabric, from selvedge to selvedge, start printing in *pink*, placing the screen far enough away from the previous print to avoid smudging. Then return to your starting point and print in the gaps.
2. Next, using the same screen, print the *brown* between and a little below the pink prints.
3. When the brown printing is completely dry, print the *beige* - this time slightly higher than the pink.

Finishing

Once all the printing has been completed, allow the ink to dry, then heat-set the fabric.

BUTTERFLIES

We have a collection of Peruvian butterflies mounted under glass at home. I removed the frame and photocopied the butterflies, enlarging my favourites. After cutting them out and arranging them, I traced the design in black ink. You could do the same with a photograph of butterflies from a wildlife magazine or book.

Additional Materials
Architectural tracing paper
Dip pen
Opaque black ink
Water colour brush: size 3
Fabric: own choice
Design: (15) on page 90

The Positive
1. On a photocopier, enlarge the butterflies on page 90 (or your own pictures) to the size you would like them to be, then cut them out and arrange them to fit into a 40 cm [15¾ in] square.
2. Place the tracing paper over the butterflies and trace them with pen and ink, then use a brush or a pen to fill in the areas which are black in the photocopies.
3. Hold the finished tracing up to the light to check that the areas that are solid black are completely opaque. (If you stick the tracing to a window, it will be easier to do the final touch-up.)

NOTE
Any lines that are finer than .7 mm [1/30 in] are difficult to expose correctly and do not print, so do not draw your lines too finely.

The Screen
1. Tape the positive onto the glass of the exposure box, then lower the sensitized screen onto it, centring it carefully. Expose the screen according to the instructions on page 66.
2. Wash out the screen following the instructions on page 67, then fill in the area of mesh between the exposed emulsion and the frame with packaging tape, filler or light-sensitive emulsion. (If you use the latter, the screen will need to be exposed again.)

The Colour
I printed the butterflies in black on white cotton and the effect was very striking, but other colours could work equally as well. Try printing deep blue on a pale blue fabric, or orange on dusty pink, or brown on khaki.

Registration
1. Spread the fabric over the printing table and, for an all-over design, mark off every 40 cm [14 in] along the width and length of the fabric, then join these points with a chalk line, so that the whole area is covered with squares. (See the instructions for registering an all-over design on page 18.)
2. Place the screen on any of the middle squares marked on the fabric and mark off two points on each side of the frame where the chalk lines intersect.

Printing
1. Working across the width of the fabric, position the screen at the bottom left-hand corner of the cut end. Spoon the ink onto the screen and print alternate squares across the fabric and alternate rows up its length as for the 'Ndebele Border' project (see page 52).
2. Return to the beginning and fill in the empty squares and rows.

Finishing
Once all the printing has been completed, allow the ink to dry, then heat-set the fabric.

My daughter had fun outlining the butterflies with silk painting fluid and then painting them with silk paints. This made a beautiful cushion cover (see above).

GUINEAFOWL

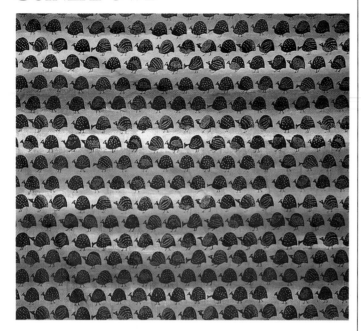

South of the Sahara, flocks of this funny bird are regularly seen pecking and trotting about on garden lawns, along the roadside, on farmlands or in nature reserves - their precision-spotted, rounded bodies an irresistible design subject.

After I had printed the 'Landscape Jacket' (see page 31), which is based on the patterns and colours of wheat fields, the idea came to me to print a lining depicting the African guineafowl.

Additional Materials
Architectural tracing paper
Rotring FL film drawing ink: black
Draughting pen
Large sheet of black paper
Masking tape
Fabric: own choice
Design: (16) on page 91

The Positive
There were 40 guineafowl in the original hand-drawn design. They are reproduced on page 91 for you to enlarge, trace and use as a basis for a design.

The Screen
It took so long to draw the guineafowl that after 40 drawings I stopped and wondered how I could fill my whole screen without having to draw any more.

I thought that if small sections could be exposed separately while the rest of the screen was covered, I could repeatedly expose the positive on the screen itself, so cutting down on printing time. It worked.

This is how it is done:
1. Take a piece of black paper large enough to cover the glass of your exposure box and, in the centre, cut out a rectangle exactly the same height as the repeat pattern (the original repeat was 13.5 cm [5$\frac{3}{8}$ in]) and 2 cm [$\frac{3}{4}$ in] wider than the positive. Tape it down on the glass.

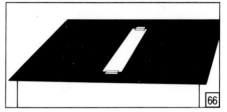

2. Tape the positive that you have drawn over this rectangle.

3. Centre the sensitized screen over the rectangle 7.5 cm [3 in] from the top edge, then stick a strip of masking tape parallel to the long edge of the black paper closest to you.
4. To move the screen up *exactly* the height of the positive for each of the exposures, make a mark on the frame 10 cm [4 in] from the corner and another mark exactly corresponding to it on the masking tape on the black paper.
5. On the screen, mark off the height of the repeat, so that it can be moved up exactly the right distance for each exposure.

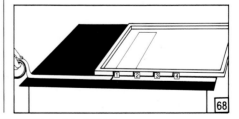

6. Pull out the shelf from the exposure box and give the screen its full exposure (see page 66) in one rectangle only.

7. Slot the shelf back into the exposure box, then, using the pencil marks as a guide, move the screen down one repeat.

8. Expose the next rectangle by pulling out the shelf.

9. Repeat this process until the screen is full. (I only fitted three repeats onto my 61 cm x 56 cm [24 in x 22 in] screen but the printing really went much faster.)

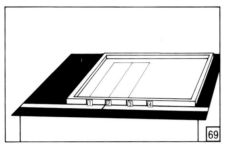

10. Wash out the screen following the instructions given on page 67, then fill in the area of mesh between the exposed emulsion and the frame with packaging tape, filler or light-sensitive emulsion. (If you use the latter, the screen will need to be exposed again.)

The Colour

I originally printed this design in brown on beige fabric to co-ordinate with the 'Landscape Jacket', but I now usually print it in a deep blue.

Originally printed as a lining for the 'Landscape Jacket', 'Guineafowl' has been one of the author's most popular fabric designs, lending itself to exciting combinations of colour for numerous fashion and interior décor applications.

For the *blue*, mix 250 ml [9 fl oz] clear base and 250 ml [9 fl oz] azure, then add 30 ml [2 tbsp] magenta and 15 ml [1 tbsp] primrose. Mix well.

Registration

To mark your fabric into a grid of rectangles measuring 40.5 cm [16 in] high (12 rows) by 39 cm [15$\frac{3}{8}$ in] wide (10 birds):

1. Spread and smooth the fabric over your printing table, then snap a chalk line 5 cm [2 in] from the lower cut edge.

2. Measure out 39 cm [15$\frac{3}{8}$ in] widths along the chalk line.

Using 120 cm-wide [48 in-wide] fabric: you will fit three repeats, leaving a 1.5 cm [$\frac{5}{8}$ in] unprinted strip down each selvedge.

Using 150 cm-wide [59 in-wide] fabric: you will still only be able to fit three repeats as it is very messy to print over the edge of the material onto the table. It is best, therefore, to leave an unprinted border of 33 cm [13 in] down one selvedge. (This fabric strip can be used for the border of another project.)

3. Mark off 40.5 cm [16 in] lengths (the height of the design) along the selvedges, then use the chalk line again to mark out the grid.

4. Place the screen over the fabric so that you can see the chalk line running through the guineafowl's feet on the bottom row of the design. Then mark your screen on the outside of the frame in the eight places where the chalk line grid passes underneath it (see diagram 7 on page 18).

Printing

Print alternate rows along the length of your table and alternate rectangles along each row. When you reach the end of the table, return to the beginning of the fabric and print the spaces.

Finishing

After the printing has been heat-set, try sponging different colours over the fabric, or cover it with melted candle wax, squeeze it into a ball to make cracks in the wax, then dye the fabric with commercial cold water dyes which are obtainable from most chemists. Another change would be to print real grasses over the guineafowl as in the 'Grasses' project (see page 68).

> **NOTE**
> You will have to measure the design on your own screen for *exact* dimensions before marking out your fabric.

POPPIES

I love the fresh colours of poppies: the yellows, oranges and pinks; their soft, fragile, crinkled petals, and their curvy, hairy stems.

In this project, one light-sensitive screen is used to print the black outline of the poppies and a second screen is used with paper stencils to print the colours. If you only have one screen it is still possible to do this project, but it means that you will have to clean the light-sensitive emulsion off to print the colours.

Additional Materials

1 clean screen (2 screens in total)
Architectural tracing paper: 3 sheets
 x 50 cm [19¾ in] square
White paper: 50 cm [19¾] square
Mapping pen
Opaque black ink
Suggested fabric: thin muslin or
 medium-weight cotton
Design (17) on page 92

NOTE
A mapping pen is very fine, so all the lines must be built up with a series of strokes.

The Positive

Using a photocopier, enlarge the design to measure 42 cm x 32 cm [16½ x 12½ in]. Place the tracing paper over it and trace the design using a mapping pen and black ink.

The Screens

SCREEN 1

1. Prepare the screen for exposure following the instructions on pages 65 or 66.
2. Expose the sensitized screen for about 2 minutes either in the sun or with a mercury vapour lamp. This is a short exposure as the lines are fine.
3. Wash out the screen (see page 67) and leave it in a warm place to dry.
4. Block off the area of mesh between the exposed emulsion and the frame with packaging tape, filler or light-sensitive emulsion. (If you use the latter, the screen will need to be exposed again.)

SCREEN 2

Take the pencil and draw a rectangle measuring 44 cm x 34 cm [17⅜ in x 13⅜ in] on the underside of the clean (non-sensitized) screen and tape around it.

The Colours

1. For the *black*, use the ink as it comes from the suppliers.
2. For the *cream*, mix 100 ml [3½ fl oz] clear base with 5 ml [1 tsp] primrose and 1.25 ml [¼ tsp] magenta.
3. For the *yellow*, mix 150 ml [5½ fl oz] clear base with 150 ml [5½ fl oz] primrose and 2.5 ml [½ tsp] magenta.
4. For the *orange*, mix 100 ml [3½ fl oz] clear base with 100 ml [3½ fl oz] primrose and 5 ml [1 tsp] magenta.
5. For the *scarlet*, mix 100 ml [3½ fl oz] clear base with 100 ml [3½ fl oz] primrose and 10 ml [2 tsp] magenta.
6. For the *green*, mix 150 ml [5½ fl oz] clear base with 10 ml [2 tsp] primrose and 2.5 ml [½ tsp] azure and 1.25 ml [¼ tsp] magenta.

The Paper Stencils

1. Tape a clean white sheet of paper onto your drawing board. Over this tape the poppy positive, and over this a clean piece of tracing paper.
2. Carefully trace all the outlines of the three flowers and the inside section of the bud.
3. Remove the top layer of tracing paper and cut out the outlined areas with your craft knife.
4. Place a clean piece of tracing paper over the poppy positive and trace the outlines of all the stems. Remove the

NOTE
The cream, yellow, orange and scarlet are fresh, clear colours and do not need the addition of their complements.

paper and cut the outlines of the stems with a craft knife. Remove the stems.

Registration

1. The design is 32 cm [12$\frac{5}{8}$ in] wide. Spread and smooth out the fabric on the printing table and measure this distance along both cut edges.

Using 120 cm-wide [48 in-wide] fabric: you will fit three repeats across, leaving a 12 cm [4$\frac{3}{4}$ in] unprinted strip down each selvedge.

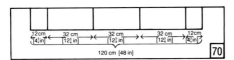

Using 150 cm-wide [59 in-wide] fabric: you will fit four repeats across, leaving an 11 cm [4$\frac{1}{2}$ in] unprinted strip down each selvedge.

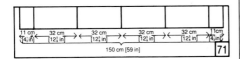

2. Snap a chalk line between the corresponding marks at each cut end of the fabric.

3. Snap a chalk line 2.5 cm [1 in] up from one of the cut edges.

4. Place the screen with the outline of the poppies on it on the lower end of the first column so that the poppy stalks are on the chalk line and the widest edges of the flowers just touch the two vertical lines.

5. Mark the four places on the screen where the vertical chalk lines intersect the top and bottom of the frame.

6. Now, from the top edge of the frame, mark off the height of the design (42 cm [16$\frac{1}{2}$ in]) up the length of the fabric on the printing table.

Printing the Black

1. The screen is in the correct position for printing, 2.5 cm [1 in] up from the cut edge of the first column. Spoon in the black ink and print.

2. Pick up the screen and, missing one mark, place the top edge of the frame on the second mark away from the first print (so that there will be a gap, equivalent to one repeat, between the first and second print that you make). Line up the two

vertical chalk lines with the marks on the top and bottom of the frame. Print the screen in this position.

3. Continue in this way printing on alternate marks until you reach the end of the column.

4. Now return to the beginning and print all the empty spaces.

5. The prints in the next columns are slightly staggered so that the repeat is not too obvious and so that the flowers are spaced out in an interesting way. (Each column of prints is started 13 cm [5 in] higher than the one next to it.)

Working in the second column, measure and mark with a fabric marking pen 13 cm [5$\frac{1}{8}$ in] up from the horizontal chalk line which runs across the cut edge. The first print in the third column will start 26 cm [10$\frac{1}{4}$ in] up and, if you are printing on 150 cm-wide [59 in-wide] fabric, the fourth column will start 39 cm [15$\frac{3}{8}$ in] up.

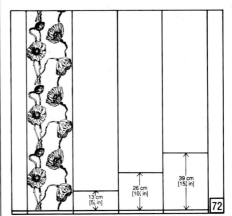

6. Place the screen in the second column so that you can see the mark that is 13 cm [5$\frac{1}{8}$ in] up from the chalk line at the bottom of the stems. Line up the marks on the top and bottom of the frame with the two vertical chalk lines. Now mark off the height of the repeat design (42 cm [16$\frac{1}{2}$ in]) up the fabric as you did in the first column and print.

7. The third column is printed in the same way, starting on the mark that is 26 cm [10$\frac{1}{4}$ in] up from the horizontal chalk line.

8. If you are printing on 150 cm-wide [59 in-wide] fabric, mark off the fourth column, starting 39 cm [15$\frac{3}{8}$ in] up from the horizontal chalk line, then print.

Printing the Colours

1. Place the paper stencil with the flowers cut out of it over the first print you made on the fabric, carefully lining it up so that the cut out areas lie directly over the printed outlines of the flowers.

2. Lower the second screen over the tracing paper stencil so that the frame surrounds the design and print in *cream*.

3. Pick any other poppy print and print the cream again. It is easy to line up the stencil with the printed outlines by simply peering through the mesh.

4. The colours on this fabric are printed randomly so that the fabric looks like a garden with flowers growing in it. In the following order print:

about 10% of the poppies in *cream*

50%	*yellow*
30%	*orange*
10%	*scarlet*

5. Peel off the paper stencil and clean the screen with a strong jet of water. (Leave on the packaging tape.)

6. For added variety and richness of colour, rub a little extra ink into the wet flowers once they have all been printed.

Using a brush or the tip of a finger, rub a little *green* over the centres of the flowers, *scarlet* over areas of orange, and *orange* over areas of yellow.

NOTE

If you are going to add colour in this way, be sure that the black outlines are *thoroughly* dry, otherwise you will smudge them. (This means that you will have to allow about four hours for the black to dry on a warm day *before* beginning to print in colour.)

---

7. Place the stencil for the stems over the first print, lining it up carefully so that the open spaces are exactly over the printed outlines.

8. Lower the clean screen over the paper stencil and print all the stems in green.

Finishing

Leave the ink to dry thoroughly, then heat-set the fabric.

This is a big design which would be suitable for curtains or duvet covers. It is also suitable as a single print on a pure white T-shirt.

'Poppies' fills this warm wooded kitchen with the freshness of spring.

PERSIAN FLOWERS

The idea for these flowers came from a 16th-century Persian brocade which caught my eye when I was browsing through a book on old textiles.

The fabric in this project is printed in four colours (pale green, dark green, pink and maroon) but only two screens are used. All the leaves, stems and centres of the flowers are printed in pale green, then parts of the mesh on the green-printing screen are painted with filler. Dark green is printed over the first pale green prints, so that on the fabric you see some of the pale green of the original print as well as the dark green which has over-printed parts of the pale green. The same process is followed with the pink and maroon.

This design is particularly striking printed with opaque textile printing inks onto cotton velvet.

Additional Materials

1 extra sensitized screen (2 in total)
Architectural tracing paper
Opaque black ink
Draughting or dip pen
Water colour brush: size 3
Filler
Fabric: own choice
Designs: (18) and (19) on page 93

AS AN ALL-OVER DESIGN

The Positives

You will need to prepare two positive transparencies: one for printing green and one for printing pink.

1. Using a photocopier, enlarge both types of bunches so that each bunch measures 14.5 cm [5¾ in] across. (You will need two of each design.)

2. Arrange your four bunches on a piece of paper 33 cm long x 36.25 cm wide [13 in long x 14⅜ in wide]. There should be two rows. The two bunches in the bottom row should be 1 cm [⅜ in] apart and close to the left-hand edge of the paper. The second (top) row of two bunches should be on the right-hand side of the paper and dovetailed 3 cm [1¼ in] in between the bunches of the lower row.

3. *The 'green' positive:* Using pen and ink, trace the outlines of all the leaves, stems and flower centres for the four bunches onto architectural tracing paper, then fill them in using a water colour brush.

4. *The 'pink' positive:* Trace, then paint in all the flowers, excluding the centres, using black ink.

The Screens

1. It is important that both positives line up in exactly the same position on each screen. To achieve this, follow the instructions for lining up designs for multi-colour printing given on page 51.

2. Expose the positive on each screen using either sunlight (see page 65) or a mercury vapour lamp (see page 66).

3. Wash out the unexposed emulsion from the screens following the instructions on page 67.

4. If you have lined up your positives as directed above, you will see that four open circles have been left by the Prestik. Just fill them in with filler or light sensitive emulsion. (If you use the latter you will need to expose the screen for a second time.)

5. Block out the open area of mesh between the emulsion and the frame with filler or light-sensitive emulsion (see Step 4 above).

The Colours

1. For the *dark green*, mix 100 ml [3½ fl oz] blue with 250 ml [9 fl oz] clear base, then add a little primrose and an even smaller amount of magenta.

2. For the *pale green*, add 100% more clear base to the first green.

3. For the *dark pink*, mix 250 ml [9 fl oz] clear base with 100 ml [3½ fl oz] magenta as the main colour, followed by tiny amounts of blue and an even smaller amount of primrose. (The addition of primrose is necessary to make the colour a little mellow.)

4. For the *pale pink,* add 100% more clear base and a little more yellow, otherwise it is very 'candy' pink.

Registration

As the repeat is a 'stepped' rectangle, it is difficult to mark out a grid on the fabric. Using 120 cm-wide [48 in-wide] fabric, I printed it as a series of borders from selvedge to selvedge.

1. Spread and smooth out the fabric on your printing table, then snap a chalk line 5 cm [2 in] up from the cut edge of your fabric.

2. Lay the screen for printing green onto the fabric so that the ends of the stems in the lower row touch the chalk line.

3. Measure the exact width of the repeat. (It should be 29 cm [$11\frac{1}{2}$ in], that is, the total width of two bunches.)

4. From the right-hand side of the screen, mark these distances off along the width of the fabric (see the instructions for registering a border on page 17).

Printing

THE 'GREEN' STENCIL

1. Print alternate sections of the first row of prints until you reach the other selvedge, then fill in the unprinted spaces. (On every alternate row it will be necessary to tape off that portion of the screen that overlaps onto the printing table.)

2. To establish the height of the next row (the second row of printing does not start immediately above the first row but dovetails in between the bunches), place a ruler across the tops of the highest leaves of the printed row and measure down 3 cm [$1\frac{1}{4}$ in]. Snap a chalk line across the fabric at this height. and print as before

THE 'PINK' STENCIL

Looking through the mesh, it is very easy to see where the flowers must be printed in pink. If the screens have been made in perfect registration as explained on page 51, use the same chalk lines on the fabric as were marked out for the first screen.

THE THIRD AND FOURTH COLOURS

When the 'green' and 'pink' stencils have been printed, the design looks acceptably complete and you could leave it like that. To add more interest, however, parts of both colours can be over-printed in a darker colour.

1. Working on the underside of the 'green' screen, paint filler over all the leaves and stalks that you want to remain pale green. Leave until the filler is completely dry.

2. Place the screen over the first pale green print and, lining it up carefully, print dark green over the pale green. You will see that the parts of the design that were blocked off with filler stopped the dark green ink printing and remain pale green.

3. Repeat this process on the 'pink' screen, blocking out those flowers you wish to remain pale pink.

Finishing

Once all the printing has been completed, allow the ink to dry, then heat-set the fabric.

> **NOTE**
> The leaf design used as a braid for the 'Persian Flowers' design is quickly printed from a paper stencil.

> **NOTE**
> As can be seen in the photograph on page 41, I printed three different patterns using the same colour scheme - 'Hawaiian Quilt', 'Little Flowers' and 'Persian Flowers' - and although they are all quite different, they co-ordinate well due to the similarity of colours.

THE T-SHIRT

I used the same design for printing the T-shirt as for printing the fabric, but this time I enlarged the bunches to measure 16 cm [$6\frac{1}{4}$ in] across. On each screen I exposed eight bunches instead of four and I arranged these in three bunches across the top and bottom rows and two in the middle. This design needs a larger screen (76 cm x 61 cm [30 in x 24 in]) but if your screen is smaller, keep the bunches the same as for the all-over design.

Additional Materials

2 sensitized screens: 76 cm x 61 cm [30 in x 24 in]

Opaque textile printing inks: sage green and shocking pink
T-shirt: black cotton knit
Hardboard: to fit inside T-shirt
Spray-on adhesive (T-fix)

The Positives

As for the all-over design you will need two positives, one for printing green and one for printing pink.

1. Enlarge each of the two bunches to 16 cm [6¼ in] in width. You will need six of the one design and two of the other.
2. On a piece of paper 48 cm long x 54 cm wide [19 in long x 21¼ in wide] place a row of three bunches along the top and another three along the bottom. In between, place the two bunches with a different design. The three rows should dovetail into each other by 4.5 cm [1¾ in].

The Screens

1. Line up the positives on the screens following the instructions for lining up designs for multicolour printing given on page 51.
2. Expose the screen using either sunlight (see page 65) or a mercury vapour lamp (see page 66).
3. Wash out the unexposed emulsion following the instructions on page 67.
4. Assuming that you have lined up your positives as directed, you will see that the Prestik has left four round 'holes' on each screen. Fill in these holes with filler or light-sensitive emulsion. (If you use the latter, the screens will need to be exposed again.)
5. Block out the area of mesh between the emulsion and the frame with filler or light-sensitive emulsion.

Printing

If the fabric is to be printed before being made up as a T-shirt, then use the printing table as usual. If, however, the design is to be printed onto a ready-made T-shirt, it will be necessary to cut a piece of hardboard to fit inside the shirt to prevent the ink sinking through to the back.

PRINTING ONTO A READY-MADE T-SHIRT:
1. Spray the hardboard with T-Fix to avoid any movement of the fabric during printing.

2. Lift up the front of the T-shirt and slide the hardboard inside, lining it up with the sides and bottom of the shirt. Then drop the front onto the sticky surface and smooth it out carefully without stretching the fabric.
3. Take the 'green' screen first and follow the directions for printing multicolour T-shirts in Method 5 on page 19.
4. Similarly, line up the 'pink' screen and print the pink.

Finishing

The T-shirt must be heat-set before being worn (a hot iron is sufficient).

Beads add textural interest to the 'Persian Flowers' design on this T-shirt.

MATTHEW'S JETS

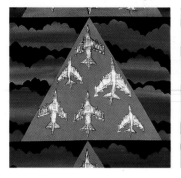

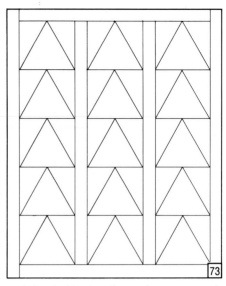

At nine years of age my son, Matthew, was very keen on jets and battles and drew amazingly small, intricate drawings. The ones printed in this project were drawn in pencil on newsprint and were only 4 cm [1⅝ in] long.

The purpose of including this project is not so that you can follow it step-by-step but to demonstrate how some of your children's drawings can easily be transformed into fabric designs.

The Positive
In order to prepare a positive using these jets they first had to be enlarged. This was done on a photocopier until the largest jet was 18 cm [7 in] long. Because the paper was not pure white, the grain became enlarged to a big speckle, so we cut out the jets close to the outline.

Next, we photocopied a few of the different sizes onto a transparent sheet.

As many of the drawings as could be accommodated were crammed onto the glass screen of the photocopier because we intended cutting them out and spacing them properly when we planned the design at home.

The Screens
We had decided that we were going to print fabric for a quilt, so I suggested that we print the aeroplanes in triangles, like the 'Flying Geese' design popularly used in patchwork (see diagram 73).

1. After sensitizing the screen, we arranged the transparent photocopies in the shape of a triangle on the underside of the screen and used sunlight to expose it.
2. Next, we took a clean screen for printing the background colour for the large

and the 'half' triangles. I drew a triangle on the mesh and then surrounded it with packaging tape.

The Colours
The lines of the enlarged drawings were quite fine and broken in the photocopy, so I decided it would be best to print them in black. Matthew then chose background colours of blues and greys.

The Fabric
The fabric was cut into strips just a little wider than the base of each triangle.

Registration
I marked the height of each triangle up each strip of fabric and snapped a chalk line across the fabric where the marks were to form a series of rectangles. The strip was then printed like a border.

Printing
1. With the light-sensitive stencil and using black ink, I printed a 'triangle' of jets in each of the rectangles.
2. Next, I wanted to print the triangle in a blue grey but I wanted the jets to remain unprinted. To solve this problem, on top of the printed jets I placed the transparent photocopies that had been trimmed to make up the positive for the light-sensitive stencil.
3. I then lowered the screen with the masked out triangle over the photocopies, lining up the base with the horizontal chalk line, and printed.

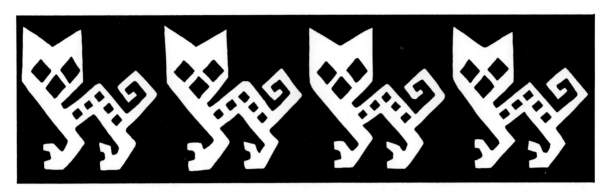

2
PERUVIAN BRAIDS : Cats
(reduced by 34%)

Centre

3
1st square

4
2nd square

Centre

3 and **4**
HAWAIIAN QUILT (reduced by 34%)

6
LEAVES
(reduced by 50%)

7
KEY DESIGN
(reduced by 34%)

9
2nd motif

10
3rd motif

8
1st motif

8, **9** and **10**
ASHANTI PRINTS
(actual size)

11
NDEBELE BORDER
(reduced by 60%)

12
NDEBELE QUILT : Square
(reduced by 34%)

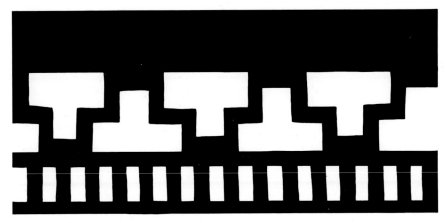

13
NDEBELE QUILT : Border
(reduced by 60%)

14
KALEIDOSCOPE
(reduced by 50%)

15
BUTTERFLIES
(reduced by 50%)

16
GUINEAFOWL
(reduced by 50%)

17
POPPIES
(reduced by 50%)

18
PERSIAN FLOWERS : Main design
(reduced by 50%)

19
PERSIAN FLOWERS : Border
(actual size)

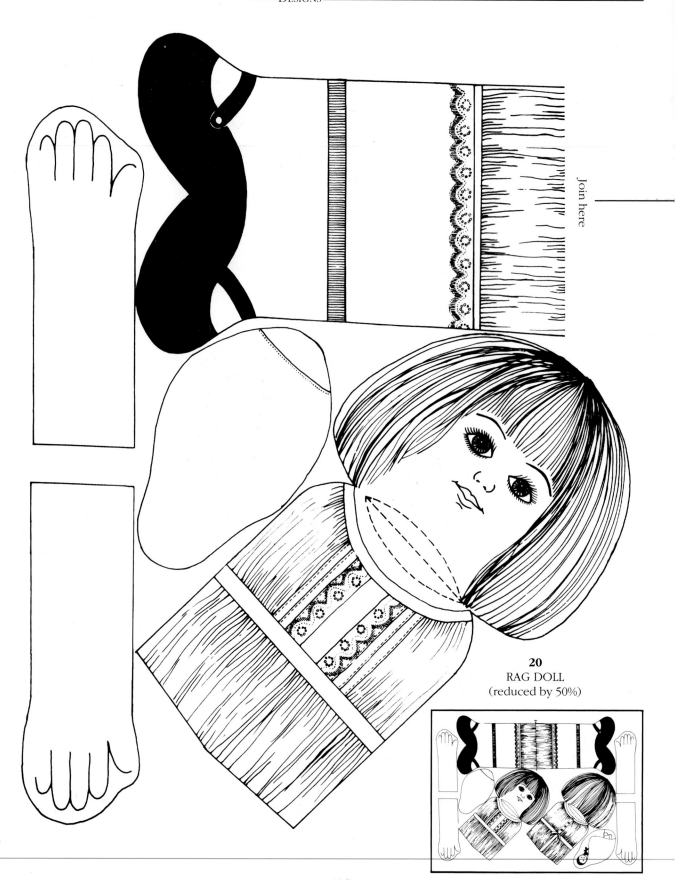

Join here

20
RAG DOLL
(reduced by 50%)